Asset Accumulation
and
Economic Activity

YRJÖ JAHNSSON LECTURES

Asset Accumulation
and
Economic Activity

Reflections on
Contemporary Macroeconomic Theory

JAMES TOBIN

THE UNIVERSITY OF CHICAGO PRESS

The University of Chicago Press,
Chicago 60637
Basil Blackwell, Oxford

Printed in Great Britain by Billing and Sons Ltd

Library of Congress Cataloging in Publication Data
Tobin, James, 1918–
   Asset accumulation and economic activity.

   (Yrjö Jahnsson lectures)
   1. Macroeconomics. I. Title. II. Series.
HB171.T6   339   80–12844
ISBN 0–226–80501–8

Contents

Preface

I had the honor to give the Yrjö Jahnsson Lectures in Helsinki in January 1978. With some revision, they appear as Chapters I, II, and IV of this book. Chapter III is a slightly amended version of the Paish lecture I gave in March 1978 at the invitation of the Association of University Teachers of Economics in York, England. The lecture has been published in the Proceedings of the Association and is reprinted here with the kind permission of the Association. The reason for including it here is that it is highly complementary to the three Jahnsson lectures.

For these reflections on current macroeconomic theory, I owe considerable intellectual debt to William Brainard, Willem Buiter, Pentti Kouri, Gary Smith, Laurence Weiss, and Janet Yellen. But of course I alone am responsible for what I said in the lectures and publish in these pages. The Cowles Foundation for Research in Economics at Yale has provided, as always, not only intellectual stimulation and guidance, but also research support of all relevant kinds. Some of the work here reported was aided by the National Science Foundation and by the American Council of Life nsurance. For help in preparing the lectures for publication I am grateful to Randall Mørck, Kathy Donahoo, and as always to my peerless secretary Laura Harrison.

Finally, I should like to express my appreciation to the Yrjö Jahnsson Foundation, my hosts in Finland, both for the opportunity to speak in their distinguished series and for their hospitality to me and my family.

New Haven
July 4, 1979

Introduction

The four lectures published here are about macroeconomic theory. These are troubled times for macroeconomics, both theory and application to policy. Our profession is deeply divided on essential points, on how to model the structures of our economies and on what government policies can improve their performance. Since the mid-1960s the degree of consensus once commanded by the post-Keynesian "neoclassical synthesis"[1] has decayed, along with confidence in the stabilizing potential of active fiscal and monetary intervention.

Many observers, economists and laymen, perceive a *crisis* in macroeconomics. Indeed the title of the now famous 1974 Jahnsson lectures of Sir John Hicks was, you will recall, *The Crisis in Keynesian Economics*.[2] But views differ

---

[1] The phrase originated with Paul Samuelson. See *The Collected Scientific Papers of Paul A. Samuelson* Vol. 2, M.I.T. Press, Cambridge, Mass., 1966, pp. 1111, 1271, 1543.

[2] J. R. Hicks, *The Crisis in Keynesian Economics*, Basil Blackwell, Oxford, 1974.

widely on the nature of the crisis, even more on the solution.

One view, prevalent among mathematical theorists of general equilibrium, is that traditional macroeconomic theory suffers from its lack of firm microeconomic foundations. The behavioral relations of macro models, it is said, are not rigorously derived from optimization by individual agents and from the clearing of markets in which optimizing agents participate. In short, macro models do not look like general equilibrium models.

Of course, it is hard to make them look like general equilibrium models without emptying the macro models of the aggregative simplicity, institutional content, and definiteness of conclusion which are their *raison d'etre*. It is possible to give macro relations the veneer of rigorous derivation from utility or profit maximization by assuming the aggregate of firms to behave as if they were one firm, and so on. Since the procedure involves a dubious assumption of aggregation, it is not clear that it is as much an improvement of the rigor and robustness of macro relations as a gratification of the trained consciences of the theorists. For some important issues of macroeconomics, to which I shall refer in these lectures, the assumption that agents are all alike is clearly not appropriate and their differences in circumstances and behavior should somehow enter the model. Candid macro economists have never deceived themselves that the equations of their models were more than simple and approximate descriptions of the diverse responses of individual agents of ever-changing relative weights in the aggregates.

In any case, the physicians who have thus diagnosed the illness of the patient have themselves sought two different cures. One group accepts, at least tentatively, what they take to be basic empirical premise of Keynesian economics, namely that prices do not continuously clear all markets.

They take for granted, then, a disequilibrium set of nominal prices, i.e., prices of goods and labor in terms of the monetary unit at which labor and other commodities would be, if agents could make all the transactions they would individually like to make, in excess supply or demand. They then investigate how, at these given prices, the movements of quantities chosen by optimizing agents, constrained by the sales and purchases they are actually able to make, will balance supplies and demand. In the same vein Keynes showed how, if interest rates and prices do not equilibrate saving and investment, variation of aggregate income will. Contributors to this theoretical development include Leijonhufvud,[3] Clower,[4] Barro and Grossman,[5] and more recently a distinguished group of French mathematical economists.[6] Edmond Malinvaud gave a masterful sum-

---

[3] A. Leijonhufvud, *On Keynesian Economics and the Economics of Keynes*, Oxford University Press, New York, 1968.

[4] R. Clower, "The Keynesian Counter-revolution: A Theoretical Appraisal," in F. Hahn and F. Brechling, eds., *The Theory of Interest Rates*, Macmillan, London, 1965.

[5] R. Barro and H. Grossman, "A General Disequilibrium Model of Income and Employment," *American Economic Review*, March 1971.

———, *Money, Employment and Inflation*, Cambridge University Press, Cambridge, 1976.

[6] Some relevant references are:

E. Malinvaud and Y. Younes, "Some New Concepts for the Microeconomic Foundations of Macroeconomics," in G. Harcourt, ed., *Microeconomic Foundations of Macroeconomics*, Macmillan, New York, 1976.

———, "Une Nouvelle Formulation Generale pour l'Etude des Fondements Microeconomiques de la Macroeconomie," to be published in *Cahiers du Seminaire d'Econometrie*, C.N.R.S., Paris.

J.-M. Grandmont, G. Laroque, and Y. Younes, "Equilibrium

mary of their work in his 1976 Jahnsson lectures.[7] I do not propose to discuss it in mine. I do notice, that for the case of excess supply of labor and other factors of production, the results closely replicate Keynesian multiplier and IS/LM analysis. The real balance effect, on which Barro–Grossman and Malinvaud rest analysis of the effects of an imposed scalar change in nominal prices, I shall be discussing in the first lecture.

The other team of diagnosticians, of which major names are Robert Lucas, Thomas Sargent, Neil Wallace and Robert Barro[8] has taken quite a different tack. They find two fatal flaws in post-Keynesian macro models. First, they too complain that the agents inside those models don't

with Quantity Rationing and Recontracting," *Journal of Economic Theory*, October 1978.

J.-P. Benassy, "Neo-Keynesian Disequilibrium Theory in a Monetary Economy," *The Review of Economic Studies*, October 1975.

[7] E. Malinvaud, *The Theory of Unemployment Reconsidered*, Basil Blackwell, Oxford, 1977.

[8] Of their numerous papers I list here only:

R. Lucas, "Understanding Business Cycles," in K. Brunner and A. Meltzer, eds., *Stabilization of the Domestic and International Economy*, Carnegie–Rochester Conference Series on Public Policy, Vol. 5, North-Holland, Amsterdam, 1977.

——, "Econometric Testing of the Natural Rate Hypothesis," in O. Eckstein, ed., *The Econometrics of Price Determination*, Washington Publications Services, Federal Reserve Board of Governors, 1972.

T. Sargent and N. Wallace, "Rational Expectations and the Theory of Economic Policy," *Journal of Monetary Economics*, April 1976.

T. Sargent, "A Classical Macroeconometric Model for the United States," *Journal of Political Economy*, April 1976.

R. Barro, "Are Government Bonds Net Wealth?", *Journal of Political Economy*, November/December 1974.

appear to be behaving rationally. The emphasis of this complaint is on the expectations of prices and other variables on which consumers, workers, firms base their current behavior. In standard models, these critics say, expectations are not based on the full information the agents should be assumed to have; they are, moreover, often biased estimates of the future values the model itself would generate. This team proposes to remedy the inconsistency in modeling by their postulate of *rational expectations*, expectations which will under stable structure be on average confirmed by events.

Second, these theorists object to the premise that markets are sometimes not cleared by prices, the very assumption the other team—the analysts of disequilibrium as constrained equilibrium—take as their working premise. Total removal of this premise from short-run macroeconomics is like taking the Prince of Denmark out of Shakespeare's play *Hamlet*. So I shall argue in my second lecture, which is devoted to the "new classical macroeconomics," the name its protagonists have given theory which combines the two assumptions of rational expectations and continuous market clearing.

The controversy which this theory has opened is a resumption of an older theoretical battle forty years ago, provoked by Keynes's challenge to the old classical macroeconomics. Then too the issues were whether and how flexibility of nominal prices clears markets, in particular whether and how flexibility of wages and prices avoids excess labor supply, i.e., involuntary unemployment. Consequently, in the first lecture I shall reconsider the real balance effect, introduced by Keynes's classical antagonist Professor A. C. Pigou.[9] This will provide background and

---

[9] A. C. Pigou, "The Classical Stationary State," *Economic Journal*, December 1943.

perspective, I hope, for looking at the challenge of the new classical macroeconomics in the second and third lectures.

The second lecture is a general critique of the new doctrines. The third concerns a particular application of them, the so-called Ricardian equivalence theorem. As recently stated by Barro, the proposition is that rational expectation of future taxes deprives debt financing of government expenditures of all macroeconomic effect. The expenditures may make a difference, but whether they are financed by borrowing or by taxation does not matter.

The fourth lecture also derives its motivation, at least in part, from recent dissatisfactions with macroeconomic theory, particulary with the standard Hicksian IS/LM apparatus as often used and interpreted. A flaw in that apparatus, it has been alleged, is that it does not respect "the government budget constraint," the obvious fact that government deficits must be financed by issuing either money or non-monetary debt. Neglect of this identity—a better word than constraint—is said to be responsible for misleading, possibly even for perverse, conclusions about the effects of fiscal policy.[10] In the fourth lecture I try to explain

---

[10] Some of the relevant references are:

C. Christ, "A Short Run Aggregate-Demand Model of the Interdependence and Effects of Monetary and Fiscal Policies with Keynesian and Classical Interest Elasticities," *American Economic Review*, May 1967.

———, "A Simple Macroeconomic Model with a Government Budget Restraint," *Journal of Political Economy*, January/February 1968.

D. Ott and A. Ott, "Budget Balance and Equilibrium Income," *Journal of Finance*, March 1965.

W. Silber, "Fiscal Policy in IS–LM Analysis," *Journal of Money, Credit, and Banking*, November 1970.

The literature has been critically reviewed by:

A. Blinder and R. Solow, "Analytical Foundations of Fiscal

how this problem is only one aspect of a general problem, that of modeling stocks and the flows that change stocks. I make a suggestion on how to handle the general problem and illustrate it by models examining the effects of macro policies in closed and open economies. On the particular question whether conventional conclusions about fiscal and monetary effects are reversed when the government budget identity is explicitly modeled, my conclusion is generally negative.

———————

Policy," *The Economics of Public Finance*, Brookings Institution, Wash., D.C., 1974.

I

Real Balance Effects Reconsidered

Keynes and Underemployment Equilibrium

Let us go back to the 1930s and to the theoretical controversy ignited by Keynes's iconoclastic *General Theory*, published in 1936.[1] Keynes claimed to have found underemployment equilibrium. The word is *equilibrium*. For Keynes was not content to assert the empirical possibility, even the likelihood, of involuntary unemployment, indeed of stubbornly persistent involuntary unemployment. That was, after all, scarcely an extravagant observation after seven years of world-wide depression and a decade of high unemployment in Britain. As a matter of theoretical principle, he went much further. The *General Theory*, particularly in its opening three chapters, denies the existence of self-correcting market mechanisms which would eliminate excess supplies of labor and other productive resources. It denies their existence, furthermore, in a competitive

---

[1] J. Keynes, *The General Theory of Employment, Interest and Money*, Macmillan, London, 1936.

economy; Keynes does not say that the mechanisms fail because of misguided government interventions in the price system—minimum wages and the like—or because of private combinations in restraint of trade—trade unions and industrial cartels. Instead he challenges orthodoxy on sacred ground, its faith that competition will so adjust prices of products and factors as to eliminate excess supplies, or demands, in all markets. He does not say merely that this process may take a very long time; he says that it does not work at all. The challenge was deliberate and explicit. The mistaken orthodoxy he described, somewhat imprecisely, as "classical" theory, and its foremost exponent he identified as his own Cambridge friend, colleague, fellow-student of Marshall, Professor A. C. Pigou. Pigou was not slow to take up the challenge.

Keynes's argument for *equilibrium* with involuntary unemployment had two strands. The first was an explanation why the price of labor—the money wage rate—did not fall in the face of excess labor supply. The second was an explanation why even if it did fall, as it should in a well-behaved competitive market, the result would not be an increase in employment. (Keynes hinted that the two points might be related, in the sense that one reason for labor resistance to wage deflation could be an intuitive appreciation of its futility.) Pigou's response was devoted primarily to the second point, and that is also the primary concern of this lecture.

As for the first point, Keynes's argument was that unemployed workers have no effective way to signal to employers their availability for work at a lower *real* wage. The money wage itself is not set in an auction market where unemployed workers can bid for jobs against each other and against employed workers. It is set by employers unilaterally or in concert with their employees, organized or unorganized: in either event, the chief concern is the wage rate relative to wages in competing firms or in comparable occupations and situations, and not the availability of cheaper workers at the factory gates. The special position of the inside work force, whether organized or not, derives from its possession, individually and collectively, of firm-specific skill and experience.

These observations, which I have liberally paraphrased, are to a considerable degree convincing. Many of them are now being formalized, in what is currently known as implicit contract theory[2] and in application of capital theory and bilateral monopoly theory to employer–employee relations. Now, as in the Depression, they explain why established wage patterns—whether they involve annual wage increases of 8 or 10% or simply downward stickiness of wage levels—are eroded only very slowly by unemployment. But they do not say that money wages will not erode at all. The same economic climate that generates high unemployment also impairs employers' ability to pay high and increasing money wages to their existing employees. Layoffs, plant closings, bankruptcies, and threats of such disasters, confront employed workers with choice between wage concessions and loss of jobs. The Great Depression, as well as the recent severe recession, provides numerous examples. Thus Keynes's first point serves better to emphasize the difficulty and slowness of melting frozen wage levels or wage-increase patterns than to establish that they never melt at all. Presumably on similar reasoning, Professor Pigou concentrated his counter-fire on the second point.

---

[2] M. N. Baily, "Wages and Employment Under Uncertain Demand," *Review of Economic Studies*, January 1974.
———, "On the Theory of Layoffs and Unemployment," *Econometrica*, July 1977.
C. Azariadis, "Implicit Contracts and Underemployment Equilibria," *Journal of Political Economy*, December 1975.

Deflation and Aggregate Demand

According to Keynes, there are theoretically conceivable and empirically important circumstances in which reduction of money wage rates would not succeed in increasing aggregate demand for goods and services. Production and employment would remain unchanged. Prices would be lower in the same proportion as wages. Real wages, real profit margins, indeed all real variables, would be unaffected. In short, the real equilibrium of the economy—unemployment and all—is independent of the level of money wages and prices. It is of course not independent of the real wage. Employers would offer more employment at a lower real wage, and workers—whether previously employed or unemployed—would be glad to accept it. But unless a reduction of the *money wage* would somehow increase aggregate *real* demand, there is no mechanism by which the mutual latent willingness to demand and to supply more labor at a lower real wage—or possibly even at the same real wage—could be actualized. This is the Keynesian impasse.

In fact, Keynes himself described one way out of the impasse, a mechanism which considerably restricted the generality which he seemed to be claiming for it in the first part of his great book. This mechanism, sometimes called the "Keynes effect," was the following: At lower money wages, prices, and incomes, supply of money would be larger in real volume or in Keynes's own wage units. The transactions demand for cash would be smaller; the excess stock of cash would bid up the prices of interest-bearing securities and lower interest rates. At lower interest rates real investment would be higher. Thus aggregate demand, further boosted by the multiplier, would expand output and employment. Hence wage and price deflation is an equivalent—a bizarre and second-best equivalent in Keynes's view—to expansionary monetary policy. If one will work, so will the other.

Here enters the famous liquidity trap, the situation in which an increase in the *real* quantity of money, whether by active central bank intervention or by deflation, will be ineffectual. This is the situation in which interest rates relevant to investment are already as low as they can go. The absolute floor for nominal interest rates is zero, the return on money itself. The effective floor, at which people will be indifferent between holding money idle and buying interest-bearing assets, might be, Keynes thought, a bit above zero. Even short term government paper would have to provide a minimal fractional gain relative to hoarding money, to compensate for transactions costs, imperfect liquidity, and risk. Long term interest rates, which could be regarded as an average of current and expected short rates, would be held above zero by expectations, or simply fears, that short rates will rise from rock bottom in future.

Like money wage patterns, such stickiness might be regarded as a disequilibrium phenomenon, in principle transient even if in practice stubborn. But all Keynes really needs anyway is the zero floor, combined with the possibility that the full employment equilibrium real interest rate—the Wicksellian natural rate that equates full employment investment and saving—is below zero. That is a possibility which, it seems, cannot be excluded by *a priori* restrictions on technology and taste.

The Pigou Effect

Or can it be? Pigou did not regard the liquidity trap impasse as particularly plausible. But he accepted it for the sake of argument, and pointed out that the real value of the wealth of the community would be increased by deflation. Money, and other assets denominated in money, are part of the public's wealth. At lower prices their purchasing power is greater, while the real value of wealth held in the form of goods is unchanged. People save to accumulate wealth to provide for their consumption, or that of their heirs, in future periods and contingencies. When the real value of their existing assets is increased, these purposes are more adequately satisfied and they will increase current consumption at the expense of saving. This is the Pigou or "real balance" effect.[3]

Pigou's first try misfired. Kalecki[4] reminded him in print that the largest part of private holdings of monetary assets, including bank deposits counted as money, had direct or indirect counterpart in private debt. Deflation raised the burden of the debts as much as the real value of the assets. As Pigou acknowledged, the correction left him with a much smaller net base. One component is the part of the public's money stock supplied directly by the government: currency and coin and their equivalent in central bank deposits held as bank reserves, the quantity currently denoted as the monetary base or high-powered money or outside money.

A possible second component is the public's holdings of non-monetary interest-bearing government obligations. Whether these, or any fraction of them, constitute net wealth has been a matter of controversy at least since

---

[3] A. C. Pigou, "The Classical Stationary State," *Economic Journal*, December 1943.

[4] M. Kalecki, "Professor Pigou on 'The Stationary State'—A Comment," *Economic Journal*, April 1944.

A. C. Pigou, "Economic Progress in a Stable Environment," *Economica*, August 1947.

Ricardo,[5] and the debate still rages today.[6] I will discuss it at some length in the third lecture. The question is whether taxpayers, anticipating that taxes will be levied to service a larger real public debt, regard themselves as poorer in the same degree as the bondowners regard themselves as wealthier. Even if the government debt is washed out on this account, the monetary base remains. So presumably do those government obligations which in the liquidity trap have become the equivalent of money, bearing zero or minimal interest. As Leontief has observed, sufficient deflation of money wages and prices can make it possible to purchase the whole GNP with one dime.[7] Presumably by then the Wicksellian natural interest rate, equating full employment saving and investment, would be well in the positive orthant and the Keynesian impasse would be escaped.

Pigou relied on the response of consumption and saving to wealth; this tradition, reinforced by Patinkin,[8] has been followed by most theorists. However, an argument with parallel import could be made that increasing the real value of monetary wealth is favorable to *investment*. Portfolio theory suggests that wealth-owners, finding themselves not only with larger wealth but with a larger share of it in

---

[5] D. Ricardo, *The Principles of Political Economy and Taxation*, E. P. Dutton, New York, 1912, pp. 161, 198–9.

[6] R. Barro, "Are Government Bonds Net Wealth?", *Journal of Political Economy*, November/December 1974.

[7] Quoted by P. Samuelson in "A Brief Survey of Post-Keynesian Developments," *Keynes' General Theory: Reports of Three Decades*, Robert Lekachman, ed., St. Martin's, New York, 1964, p. 333.

[8] D. Patinkin, "Price Flexibility and Full Employment," *American Economic Review*, September 1948; and in *Money, Interest and Prices*, 2nd ed., Harper and Row, New York, 1965.

monetary form, will wish to shift towards goods or equities. Thus they may lower the effective yields required of investments in consumers' or producers' durable goods, relative to those available on money and Treasury bills or bonds. This change in the structure of interest rates could be favorable to investment even if rates on secure liquid nominally denominated assets were stuck in the trap.

The Pigou effect breaks the correspondence between deflation and monetary policy. Keynes could no longer say that anything deflation can do, monetary policy can do (and can do with less trauma). He could say—though I don't think he did, busy as he was with practical affairs—that the Pigou effect of deflation could be duplicated by fiscal policy, specifically by government spending or tax reduction financed by printing money. That would not only provide direct fiscal stimulus but also, like Pigou's deflation, add to the public's wealth and specifically to its monetary component.

In some modern minds, the question may arise how in either case wealth is increased in any meaningful sense. From a larger perspective, does not the wealth of a nation consist of its real productive assets, human and nonhuman? These are what an outside observer, say in a space satellite with a powerful telescope, would enumerate and value. (I and he leave aside claims on the rest of the world. The argument concerns a closed economy; Keynes did not contest the traditional view that deflation could work for a small open economy with a fixed exchange rate.) How can a nation make itself richer either by printing pieces of paper or by increasing their value by charging each other fewer of them in exchanges of goods and services? The answer, I think, is in two parts. First, the social contrivance of commonly acceptable money, facilitating contemporaneous and intertemporal exchange, is of social value to the nation collectively as well as to holders individually. Its contribution to national wealth may well depend on its aggregate amount. Second, in the particular situation under discussion, it is only a breakdown—whether temporary or permanent—in *internal* arrangements which is responsible for failure to use fully the real productive assets of the economy. If additional monetary assets remedy the breakdown, the real national wealth they represent is the value of the resulting stream of gains in production and consumption.

Irving Fisher on Deflation and Debt

Earlier in the same Great Depression another great economist, Irving Fisher, had reached a diagnosis precisely the opposite of Pigou's.[9] Fisher thought that reflation, not deflation, was the remedy. He was struck by the increased burden that lower prices imposed on debtors—corporations, proprietors, home-owners, farmers. Debt squeezes, defaults, and bankruptcies, he thought, intensified and spread the slump in economic activity. He urged measures—monetary expansion, devaluation, marking up gold prices—designed to restore commodity prices to pre-Depression levels. For Fisher in 1932–3, more even than Keynes in 1936, raising prices was a step indispensable to recovery, not just an incidental byproduct of other measures.

I recall Fisher's position not solely from Yale patriotism but to bring our attention back to the casual "washing out" of private debts and credits in the reckoning of the base for

---

[9] I. Fisher, "The Debt Deflation Theory of Great Depressions," *Econometrica*, October 1933, p. 337.

——, *100% Money*, Adelphi, New York, 1936, especially pp. 119–34.

the Pigou effect. The gross amount of these "inside" assets was and is orders of magnitude larger than the net amount of the base. Aggregation would not matter if we could be sure that the marginal propensities to spend from wealth were the same for creditors and debtors. But if the spending propensity were systematically greater for debtors, even by a small amount, the Pigou effect would be swamped by this Fisher effect.

There are indeed reasons for expecting, or at least for suspecting, just that. The population is not distributed between debtors and creditors randomly. Debtors have borrowed for good reasons, most of which indicate a high marginal propensity to spend from wealth or from current income or from any liquid resources they can command. Typically their indebtedness is rationed by lenders, not just because of market imperfection but because the borrower has greater optimism about his own prospects and the value of his collateral, or greater willingness to assume risk and to die insolvent, than the lender regards as objectively and prudently justified. Business borrowers typically have a strong propensity to hold physical capital, producers' durable goods. Their desired portfolios contain more capital than their net worth—they like to take risks with other people's money. Household debtors are frequently young families acquiring homes and furnishings before they earn incomes to pay for them outright; given the difficulty of borrowing against future wages, they are liquidity-constrained and have a high marginal propensity to consume.

When nominal prices and wages are deflated, debt service is a higher proportion of debtors' incomes, and the reduction or elimination of their margins of equity disqualifies them from further access to credit. Bankruptcies and defaults do likewise, and transmit the distress of debtors to their creditors, threatening the solvency and liquidity of individual lenders and financial institutions. Debtor corporations, their equity positions impaired, give priority to restoration of financial structure above real investment. The declines in real market value of their equities due to the greater burden of their debts far surpass the gains to creditors. These items in the Fisher scenario may well overshadow the positive effects of the increased real value of creditors' nominal assets.

These considerations do not apply solely to ancient history. Imagine the distress which would occur if debtors who have borrowed in the 1970s in anticipation of continued inflation were suddenly to find themselves confronted by price stability. Maybe Leontief is right that sufficient deflation would make existing coins capable of buying the whole GNP. It would also make existing debts an astronomical multiple of the GNP.

Short and Long Run Effects of Prices on Aggregate Demand

To give Pigou and Fisher each his due, I am led to make a distinction between the "long run" consequences of deflation and the "short run." Perhaps the Pigou effect applies to the first, the Fisher effect to the second. I am sure that Pigou himself was conscious of this distinction, for he entitled his final contribution to this subject "The Classical Stationary State." His successors have been less careful, confidently stressing real balance effects in short-run macroeconomic analysis.

To understand the long run Pigou effect, we must use our imagination and carry out a counter-historical "as if" experiment. Imagine two alternative histories of the same economy, over the same period of time. A common feature of the two histories is the nominal value of the monetary base at each point in time; this is the same in history I and history II. At the outset and for an extended period thereafter both economies are in a liquidity trap and are suffering unemployment. During this period nominal wages and prices are 50% lower in history II than in history I, though real wages, other relative prices, and real quantities are in the beginning the same. The period lasts long enough for all debts earlier contracted to mature and to be repaid or recontracted; alternatively, all debts outstanding were contracted with foreknowledge of the prices in each history. Pigou would say that history II would show higher employment and output than history I and would reach full employment sooner. I agree.

Unexpected price reduction in a single history—low prices following high prices sequentially—is an entirely different matter. Contracts made when prices were higher and expected to be higher remain in force. Fisher's observations apply. It would take a very long time before such contracts were worked off, and even then the economy would not be the same as if they had never existed.

Prices and Output in Short-run Macro Models

At this point, I would like to make a mildly technical digression. If, as I suspect, Fisher was very likely right about the short run effects of movements of price *level* on aggregate real demand, what does this imply for short-run macro models? Does it mean that the IS curve in r-Y space shifts upward as the price level rises in cyclical expansion? That the IS curve in r-p space for a given level of output, e.g. the full employment level, is upward sloping? Before drawing these conclusions we should remember a short-run price level effect of much greater importance now than in Fisher's time. This is the progressive structure of taxation relative to *nominal* incomes and profits; during a short run before legislative adjustment, the fact that taxes are a larger share of given real income at higher prices works in Pigou's direction. But even if the Fisher effect is stronger, and the answers to the questions above about the relation of IS loci to price levels are affirmative, this does not mean that the IS and LM loci jointly yield a positive rather than negative association of Y and p for given settings of policy. The Keynes effect—the fact that a given nominal supply of money is smaller in real value the higher the price level—still works in the conventional direction. Particularly at high levels of output and interest, far from the liquidity trap, it may well dominate any direct price level effects on wealth and spending. The curvature of the liquidity preference schedule, then, contributes asymmetry to the situation. Altogether, aggregate demand could be positively related to price level at low levels of output and interest rates but negatively related closer to full employment. This does open some possibility of multiple equilibria.

The situation can be analyzed with the help of some diagrams. In Figures 1–3, LM and IS loci are drawn for given values of the nominal money stock M and of real national product Y. They represent combinations of interest rate and price level consistent on the one hand with monetary balance, and on the other hand, with balance in demand and supply of goods. Figure 1 shows the conventional story, including the Pigou effect. The LM locus is upward sloping: the real stock of money is lower when the price level is higher, and it takes a higher interest rate to induce the public to handle transactions with smaller cash holdings. The IS locus is downward sloping: according to the conventional Pigou effect, a higher price level means less demand for goods and services, and it takes a lower interest rate to offset this effect. As the diagram also says, expansionary monetary policy "M" shifts LM to the right, while expansionary fiscal policy "F" shifts IS upwards. An

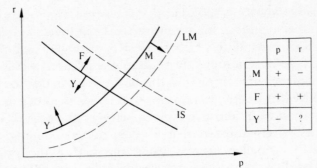

FIG. 1   conventional Pigou effect (given M, Y)

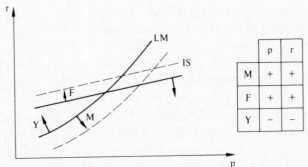

FIG. 2   reverse Pigou effect, case I (given M, Y)

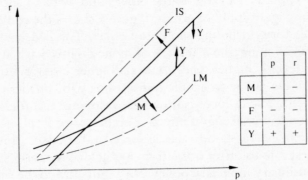

FIG. 3   reverse Pigou effect, case II (given M, Y)

increase in Y shifts LM up (more demand for money at any given P) and shifts IS down (assuming the marginal propensity to spend is less than 1). The effects on p and r are also summarized in the accompanying table.

Figures 2 and 3 show a reverse Pigou effect or Fisher effect. The IS locus is upward sloping, because the spending by debtors encouraged by higher p exceeds the spending by creditors deterred. In Figure 3 the effect is so great that IS is steeper than LM, and the comparative statics of monetary and fiscal policy are reversed.

Figures 4 and 5 are special cases of Figures 1 and 3, in

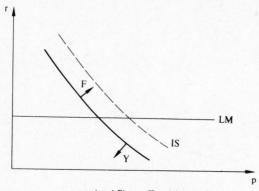

FIG. 4   conventional Pigou effect (given r, Y)

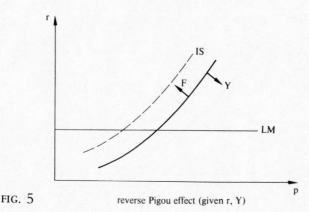

FIG. 5   reverse Pigou effect (given r, Y)

which the Keynes effect is eliminated. This would apply in the liquidity trap, or in the event of an accommodative monetary policy that pegged the interest rate. Note that in Figure 5, as in Figure 3, p and Y are positively rather than negatively associated.

Figures 1–5 have two uses. A direct application is to the classical flexible price world with real output Y supply-determined. Reversing the Pigou effect alters some traditional comparative static results. An indirect application is to the Keynesian world of demand-determined Y. This is done in Figures 6 and 7. The first panels of Figures 6 and 7

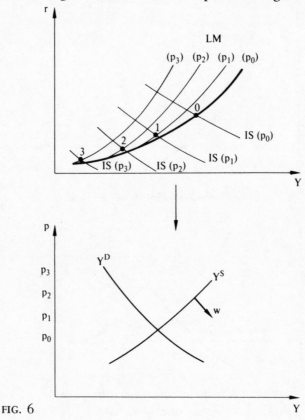

FIG. 6

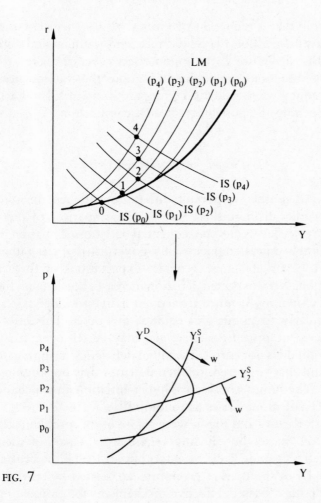

FIG. 7

show IS and LM loci in traditional (Y, r) space. Each locus assumes M and p, but a family of curves are drawn for various values of p, $p_0 < p_1 < p_2 \ldots$. The various IS/LM solutions, numbered in the panel, are translated into the second panel, where they form the Y^D relations. In Figure 6 this has the expected downward slope, implying for example that a reduction of money wages (depicted as a downward shift of Y^S) would raise employment and output. But in Figure 7, the Pigou effect reversal makes Y^D change directions, rendering ambiguous the consequences of a money wage reduction (compare shifts of Y^S_1 and Y^S_2) and opening the possibility of dual equilibrium (Y^S_1).

Conclusion for Theory and Policy

There is another important difference between the two cases earlier distinguished, the "as if" comparison of alternative price levels and the sequential deflation. Deflation in real time—unless engineered by governmental fiat rather than by markets—may generate expectations of further deflation. Now expected deflation increases the demand for money, making it more attractive relative to other assets, particularly to goods and equities in goods. This effect counters the price *level* effect and may be stronger. If so, deflation does not correct the initial deficiency in aggregate demand that triggered it. Then deflation has no stopping point. The symmetrical case is hyper-inflation, in which the velocity of money rises astronomically.

Both Keynes and Pigou were aware of this problem as a practical matter but did not regard it as a part of their theoretical game. They were too purist. Recall the central issue: Does the market economy, unassisted by government policy, possess effective mechanisms for eliminating general excess supply of labor and productive capacity? This question applies to real time and to sequential processes. Therefore the static long run "Pigou effect" does not entitle anyone to give a positive answer.[10]

---

[10] J. Tobin, "Keynesian Models of Recession and Depression," *American Economic Review, Papers and Proceedings*, May 1975.

This does not mean that Keynes wins the more abstract battle of theoretical principle. He did not show the existence of an excess-supply *equilibrium*, at least not in the meaning of the magic word equilibrium in the classical, or neoclassical, economics he was criticizing. In that meaning, equilibrium is a stationary state, and a state in which expectations are fulfilled. A sequence in which wages and prices are falling, and in which debts are embarrassing debtors who never anticipated prevailing wages and prices, is not such a state. Pigou succeeds in restricting "equilibrium" to situations in which markets clear, and Keynes's proposed equilibrium with involuntary unemployment does not qualify.

But why should Keynes care about such semantics? His important message was that Pigou's equilibrium may not be globally stable, that even if it is stable, disequilibrium can be protracted and stubborn. The forces which lower money wages and prices are slow and weak, and those which translate deflation or disinflation into greater real demand are uncertain. As Keynes also knew, protracted under-production and under-utilization severely damages the marginal efficiency of capital. In mild and short-lived recessions investment is buoyed by belief that high employment and prosperity are the long-term norm. Once this confidence is destroyed, as contemporary events again demonstrate, it is terribly difficult to revive it. The practical moral is that active policy, along with market response, is part of the social mechanism for maintenance or restoration of equilibrium.

II
Policies, Expectations, and Stabilization

In the previous lecture I recounted, with critical perspective, the Keynes–Pigou controversy of the 1930s.

The controversy of the 1930s is being replayed today. The issues are basically the same. The contestants are of course different. Just as the Keynesian revolution challenged the then prevailing orthodoxy of economic theory and policy, so the counter-revolution now challenges Keynesian orthodoxy, both theory and policy. What is called "the new classical macroeconomics"[1] attempts to explain the economic world in strikingly different terms from the post-Keynesian "neoclassical synthesis" of the 1950s and 1960s, with radically divergent policy implications. Though the lines of battle are drawn on the same issues as in the 1930s, the new classical economists have more modern and powerful armament. In the contest for the minds of economists, policy-makers, and the general

---

[1] See, for example, the contributions of Lucas, Sargent, Wallace, and Barro cited above, p. xii.

public, they have the advantage which the Keynesians had in the 1930s, namely a recent history of unsatisfactory economic performance and a general impression—right or not—that policies and prediction based on opposing doctrines have gone wrong.

This is not the first or only intellectual reaction to Keynesian macroeconomics. An earlier and still very influential counter-revolution is monetarism as expounded by Milton Friedman[2] and others. But the current movement is theoretically and politically a more sweeping departure, and in many respects it is an alternative to monetarism as well as to Keynesian macroeconomics. Monetarism Mark I said that, as between fiscal and monetary policies, only money really matters; the new classical macroeconomics says that no macroeconomic policy systematically alters the real course of the economy. Monetarism Mark I favored stable monetary growth above other monetary rules; the new doctrine implies that any predictable policy will have the same real consequences as any other. Monetarism Mark I endorsed floating exchange rates; the new position is that the exchange rate regime does not affect real outcomes. Monetarism Mark I acknowledged that shocks, other than those administered by government policy, could displace the economy for significant periods from full employment or from the "natural rate of unemployment." It agreed with the Keynesians that discretionary policy could work in principle but disagreed about their practical necessity and

---

[2] Among the many references are:

M. Friedman (ed.), *Studies in the Quantity Theory of Money*, University of Chicago Press, Chicago, 1956.

——, *The Optimum Quantity of Money and Other Essays*, Aldine, Chicago, 1969.

——, "A Theoretical Framework for Monetary Analysis," *Journal of Political Economy*, March/April 1970.

desirability. The new school denies disequilibrium and denies that policies can help or speed the natural processes of stabilization. There are of course many affinities between the two brands of monetarism. But in methodology and theoretical approach, it is not farfetched to say that both earlier monetarist macroeconomics and Keynesian macroeconomics are under attack.

The two pillars of the new classical macroeconomics are *rational expectations* and *continuous market-clearing*. Of the two, I shall argue, it is the second which is crucial for the far-reaching implications of the doctrine.

I shall be critical of these trends in economic theory and therefore I should express my respect and admiration for their authors. Their innovations in analytic technique and econometric method are powerful, and it is no wonder that they excite some of the best young minds of our profession, just as Keynesian theory and the early stirrings of econometrics excited my own generation. The more thoughtful among them, moreover, recognize that they face a formidable task, only just begun, in explaining in their terms the standard facts of economic fluctuations which Keynesian models appear to fit.

Expectations and Macro-economic Theory

I begin with some observations on the knotty problem of doing justice, in our models of economic process, to the unending linkages between current and future values of economic variables. We know, for example, that the price of any commodity or asset today depends on its price tomorrow and tomorrow and tomorrow, and on other future prices, and thus on the determinants of these prices. This is obviously true for durable goods, common stocks, land and other natural resources, bonds of long maturity. It is even true of perishable goods, given that buyers and sellers may one way or another substitute production or consumption at one time for production or consumption at another time. How can we possibly explain or describe the state of the economy today, or predict it for tomorrow, unless we can do so for all future time?

Theorists have long recognized the problem. The abstract solution, encompassing the uncertain future within the friendly confines of Walrasian general equilibrium, was proposed by Arrow and Debreu.[3] They simply multiplied the number of commodities to be traded by specifying the date and the contingency—"state of nature"—in which each good would be delivered. They also assumed each agent to have a vector of endowments of commodities so defined and a utility function over such commodities. At the beginning of economic time, a single market in these commodities, i.e., in contingent futures, determines everything; the famous Walrasian auctioneer has a big job finding the equilibrium, but he has to perform only once. The usual assumptions, applied to this extended list of commodities, guarantee the existence of equilibrium and, with the usual reservations, its optimality. Once all the contracts are made, economic life is simply the routine of fulfilling the contracts as the specified dates and contingencies occur.

The service the authors have rendered us in this ingenious construction is to show how impossible it is for the economy, and for economists, to cope with the future. In their construction, the list of commodities—hence of

---

[3] K. Arrow, "Le role de Valeurs Boursieres pour la Repartition la Meilleure des Risques," *Econometrie*, Paris, Centre National de la Recherche Scientifique, 1953.
G. Debreu, *Theory of Value*, Wiley, New York, 1959.

contingencies and dates—must be known.[4] The agents must be immortal, or somehow commitments must be made by and for the unborn. The states of nature must be defined so that the agents have no way to influence their occurrence or non-occurrence—the problem of moral hazard. There are inevitably, in any event, too many commodities to sustain credibility for the necessary assumption that their markets all exist and are purely competitive. Observe the paucity of futures markets, not to say contingent futures markets, even in highly sophisticated economies.

Obviously we do not live in an Arrow–Debreu world. Rational expectations theory may be regarded as an attempt to meet the problem that motivated the Arrow–Debreu construction and to approximate the Arrow–Debreu conclusions without postulating the unrealistically elaborate set of markets for contingent future deliveries.

Economic theory has always required realization of expectations—the expected point values or estimated probability distributions on which market behavior is based—as a *steady state equilibrium* condition. To turn the point around, the condition is that people expect what actually happens. Certainly it makes no sense to postulate a steady state in which agents fail to learn from experience and persistently act on forecast that prove erroneous. Rationality of expecta-

---

[4] On the extension of the original finite model to infinite space, see:

T. Bewley, "Equilibrium Theory with an Infinite-dimensional Commodity Space," Ph.D. dissertation, University of California at Berkeley, 1970.

——, "Existence of Equilibria in Economies with Infinitely Many Commodities," *Journal of Economic Theory*, June 1972.

——, "Equality of the Core and the Set of Equilibria in Economies with Infinitely Many Commodities and a Continuum of Agents," *International Economic Review*, June 1973.

tions in this limited sense is nothing new. Nor is it necessary to assume any particular process of expectation formation. Imagining that agents know and solve the model of the economy itself will meet the requirement. But so will adaptive or regressive rules.

Keynesian theory in its original formulation was open to criticism on this score. For example, the "speculative motive" for liquidity preference assumed long term interest rates were held up by expectations that short rates would return to normal levels. Though possibly realistic, this explanation was inconsistent with an equilibrium implying stable short term interest rates and stable calculations of marginal efficiency of capital. That is, incidentally, why I proposed an alternative theory of liquidity preference free of the inconsistency between actual and expected interest rates.[5]

Outside of steady states, the meaning of consistent or rational expectations is much less definite. Observed outcomes do not provide a sample of observations from stationary probability distributions for the values of variables. They do not even provide a sample of replicated observations of the structure that has generated the outcomes. Even if the structure is stable, a fact of which neither model-builders nor econometricians nor real-world agents can be sure, the observations are influenced by exogenous shocks difficult to identify. Shocks may occur in policies, or in other exogenous events. The shadow of the future and of the future's future also affects current outcomes. Even if, as the model-builder may assume, the agents in the economy believe the model itself, this consistency does not guarantee that the agents agree with each other regarding the nature

---

[5] J. Tobin, "Liquidity Preference as Behavior Toward Risk," *Review of Economic Studies*, February 1958.

and probabilities among various future shocks. Arrow-
–Debreu markets enforce consistency among individual
plans for future contingencies. No process of expectation
formation can achieve equivalent coordination.

Economic theorists become so accustomed to writing
into their equations symbols representing expected future
values of variables that they come to vest the symbols with a
palpable reality they do not have. The spot price of a precisely defined commodity, say a tube of a certain toothpaste
at a certain store on a specific day, has at least in principle a
single observable value. The expectation of that price a
month or a year or ten years ahead does not. Any one
individual may have a subjective probability distribution of
such a variable. The mean of his distribution presumably
exists, although his priors may be so flat over a wide range
that the mean has little significance. But there are many
individuals, and there is no reason to expect their probability distributions or their expected values to agree.

Theorists may postulate that disagreement is impossible,
because rational people with the same information are
bound to come to the same conclusion. There is plenty of
evidence that expectations are diffuse; perhaps it indicates
irrationality, perhaps differences in information, perhaps
failure of the theorists' postulate. In any event it presents a
serious problem. Whose expectation, or what combination
of diverse explanations, is represented by the single symbol
in the model?

The question is not just nit-picking. Transactions—if not
in toothpaste, then surely in financial instruments—occur in
large part because of disagreements. It follows that the
expectations of the *marginal* buyers or sellers are those that
matter in the determination of prices in spot and futures
markets. A relevant American saying is, "It takes differences of opinion to make horse races," i.e., otherwise there
would be no betting. But the marginal transactors are not

the same from day to day or year to year, and they do not necessarily represent the average opinion of market participants and non-participants. A disquieting feature of aggregate models which assume uniform expectations is that they don't explain why there are any transactions at all in existing assets.

Rational expectations as formulated in such models assume further that the statistic of an agent's probability distribution relevant to his behavior is the arithmetic mean. Yet the essential message of previous theorizing on behavior under uncertainty is that this is rarely optimal strategy. There is not in general a linear marginal relationship between future market prices or other stochastic variables and the payoffs, in utility or profit, to the decisionmaker. If there is a certainty-equivalent which can assume the role of a single-valued variable in describing behavior related to uncertain future variables, it is not necessarily the mean. Once again, individuals undoubtedly differ widely in these respects, for example in degrees of risk aversion, even if they happen to agree in subjective estimates of probabilities. These differences, too, motivate transactions which are otherwise inexplicable, for example insurance contracts with actuarially excessive premiums.

An important and intractable uncertainty is the unpredictability of the future expectations of other agents. About these expectations it seems virtually impossible to form rational expectations. Your expectations will decisively determine the values of my assets in the future, perhaps just at the moment I must consume my wealth. Consider, in particular, assets—whether paper or real—of durability longer than the life expectancy of an investor. Every generation must accumulate such assets to provide for old age. The assets are not themselves edible or otherwise consumable; their purchasing power in retirement depends on the prices the next generation will pay for them. Those prices in turn depend on, among other things, the prices the young expect their young will later pay for them. And so on, *ad infinitum*. For certain stores of value—gold, works of art, rare coins, Swiss francs—there is no intrinsic value and only an infinite regress of expectation. Even reproducible assets like durable goods, or assets like land and securities bearing marketable yields, depend on speculative valuations.

One of Keynes's many insights was his perception of these essential indeterminacies. His parable of the stock market,[6] a beauty contest where the prize goes to the entrant whose judgment most corresponds to other entrants' judgments, is a dramatic illustration. More serious, perhaps, was his insistence that the marginal efficiency of capital is as much psychological as technological. Business confidence, he thought, is in the end a partially autonomous determinant of investment and economic activity rather than a state wholly derivable from current and past economic conditions. In today's context he would say it is not capable of description as rational expectation.

In empirical practice the exponents of rational expectations seldom derive expectations strictly in the manner their methodological principles dictate. Except in the simplest models, it is indeed very difficult to find the paths along which expectations, formed by solution of the model itself, are realized. The popular shortcut is autoregression—predicting, and assuming that agents predict, a variable by regression of its current value on its own lagged values. Since this calculation does not utilize the inter-variable structure of the model, it is an *ad hoc* procedure whose superiority to other one-variable *ad hoc* procedures is far from obvious.

I do not make these points to argue that the conventional treatments of expectations in macro models, theoretical or

---

[6] *General Theory*, p. 156.

econometric, are satisfactory or superior to "rational expectations" methods. I suspect the opposite is true. My conclusions are instead these: Economists, all of us, should pay more attention to actual data on expectations and how they are formed and less to our own assumptions about what they are and how they are or should be formed. The rational expectations theorists have properly raised our consciousness of deficiencies in the modeling of expectations. But they have claimed much too much for their remedies, given the intrinsic difficulties of the subject.

Endogenous Expectation and the Effectiveness of Policies

Probably the most striking propositions of the "rational expectations" school concern the consequences of expectations about policies.[7] Some of the points are, it is true, neither controversial nor new. Among them are, for example, the common sense observation that the expected duration of a tax or tax cut or tax credit affects its economic impact. A more general point well taken is that the structure of economic behavior, including response to policy, depends upon expectations about policy. Estimates or descriptions of structure derived from observations under one regime of policy will frequently become obsolete if the *modus operandi* and objectives of policymakers change. Policy multipliers calculated from the obsolete structure will, to the confusion of econometricians and to the dismay of policymakers, prove inapplicable in the new regime.

Several examples can be offered: The statistical

---

[7] R. Lucas, "Econometric Policy Evaluation: A Critique," in K. Brunner and A. Meltzer, *The Phillips Curve and Labor Markets*, Carnegie-Rochester Conference Series on Public Policy, Vol. 1, North-Holland, Amsterdam, 1976.

regularities observed between unemployment and inflation rate in pre-1966 Phillips curves, did not survive when
economic policy attempted, whether purposefully or not,
to purchase lower unemployment with the predicted
increment of inflation. This is the favorite example of the
school. Another example is this: The statistical regularities
observed between money stock and total spending,
observed in a period when the monetary authorities were
generally oriented to interest rates and credit conditions
rather than to monetary aggregates, became less reliable
when the authorities become more monetarist and tried to
exploit them. This one is *not* a favorite example of the
school. In a more diffuse way, the behavior of business
investors and other economic agents was quite different in
the mid-1960s when they thought that active macro policy
would keep the economy at high employment and steady
real growth from what it was before and, for that matter,
from what it is now when they perceive that anti-inflation
objectives have taken priority.[8]

The stronger and more controversial proposition is that
government policies expected and understood have no real
effect, because optimizing private agents will offset them in
order to remain at their preferred positions. As a general
proposition, it does not make sense. In a chess opening, for
example, I may foresee accurately my opponent's sequence
of responses; that does not deprive his moves of their effectiveness.

One can think of cases where the proposition is true. The
city government provides downtown parking lots and
charges economic fees; merchants and private entre-
preneurs simply provided fewer parking lots. It is much

---

[8] M. N. Baily, "Stabilization Policy and Private Economic
Behavior," *Brookings Papers on Economic Activity*, 1:1978.

easier to think of cases where it is not true, where the government consumption or investment is not a perfect substitute for private goods or is provided in greater amounts than the market has or will produce, or where the program together with its financing involves redistributional and allocative effects. These are, of course, not the kinds of macro policies to which the proposition is directed.

As for fiscal policy, the argument concerns the effectiveness, for good or evil, of substituting bond finance for taxation. The question is whether any net private saving will be absorbed. An old argument attributed to Ricardo, now revived under the rational expectations banner, is that the taxes are merely being deferred.[9] The private sector will not regard itself as wealthier by acquiring bonds whose interest and principal will just suffice to pay the taxes that will be levied to service them. The "neo-Ricardian" proposition ignores some possible real effects: taxpayers and bondholders are not identical in behavior; taxpayers who are liquidity-constrained will be delighted to have their taxes deferred at the government's borrowing rate: taxes are not lump-sum but have well-known allocational incentives and disincentives; the uncertainties of the values on which taxes will be levied mean that they will be discounted at a different, probably higher rate, than the future payments to bondholders; citizens who anticipate no personal descendants or care nothing for the welfare of future generations will be glad to defer taxes. This issue is discussed at length in the next lecture.

But let us turn to money. Here the argument seems stronger. Perhaps the intended proposition is that only if the government does something *real* can it have real effects.

---

[9] R. Barro, "Are Government Bonds Net Wealth?", *Journal of Political Economy*, November/December 1974.

Money is not real. So people can remain at their preferred real positions, however much money the government supplies, simply by scaling up all nominal prices proportionately, relative prices remaining unchanged. Is this not what they will do, via private markets? Is this not what they will do coincident with additional money supply if they anticipate it correctly?

There are two fallacies in affirmative answers to these questions. The larger one concerns the effects of an anticipated step-up in the rate of growth of money supply. Suppose that this does indeed carry with it expectations of commensurately higher price inflation. That is a real change. The real rate of return on at least one asset (money) is reduced, and this is bound to affect other real rates and through them relative prices and quantities. The second applies also to a one-shot injection of money and concerns the method by which it occurs. Suppose it is base money, printed to finance government purchases of goods or tax reductions or to repurchase or retire government bonds. Those uses all have real effects, as do the changes in private wealth and its composition resulting from the transaction. If it is bank money, the same observations apply to the transactions the central and private banks must make to create it. The only neutral way to engineer a change in the quantity of money, neutral whether anticipated or not, is trivial; it is to decree a scalar change in the monetary unit of account, making old francs into centimes and one hundred old francs into new francs. It is trivial and neutral because it applies not just to the currency but to all assets and debts denominated in the unit of account.

Continuous Market Clearing: the Crucial Issue

The great economist, political theorist, and social scientist

Joseph Schumpeter, my teacher, liked to say that Leon Walras[10] gave economics its *magna carta*.[11] This was his demonstration that the economy could be regarded as solving a system of simultaneous market-clearing equations in a like number of "unknown" prices. Walras's vision was indeed powerful. In the hands of subsequent theorists it has been refined and made rigorous. Combined with the assumption that buyers and sellers are optimizing at the market prices, it has normative as well as positive implications. Schumpeter himself used the Walrasian equilibrium only as a reference point for the destabilizing departures he regarded as the essential story of capitalism.

In any case, contemporary classical theorists are bolder than their predecessors in assuming that the economic world can be described in terms of continuous clearing in competitive markets of supplies and demands derived from utility and profit maximization. This surge of confidence is not based, so far as I can see, on new empirical evidence for the assumption. It is based rather on the feeling that this model is the "only game in town." In other words, if you have lost your purse on a street at night, look for it under the lamppost. Older theorists, even Pigou, were more cautious. While they may have believed that there were strong tendencies toward the Walrasian equilibrium, they did not expect that markets were simultaneously clearing every moment of time. They were willing to acknowledge that the system was generally in disequilibrium, perhaps en route from one Walrasian solution to another. They did not think that economic theory could place very informative

---

[10] L. Walras, *Éléments d'Économie Politique Pure: ou Théorie de la Richesse Sociale*, Libraire Générale de Droit et de Jurisprudence, Paris, 1952 (1st ed., 1874).

[11] J. Schumpeter, *History of Economic Analysis*, Oxford University Press, New York, 1954, p. 242.

restrictions on the adjustment behavior of individuals and markets out of equilibrium. Contrast the new neo-classical macroeconomics, where the dynamics are those of moving equilibrium, not of disequilibrium adjustment.

We must therefore remind ourselves how severe a draft on credulity is the literal application of the market-clearing idea. The Walrasian Auctioneer is a great myth; I emphasize both words. She must collect all the demand and supply schedules for the m commodities from the n agents. She must solve the simultaneous equations, announce the market clearing prices, and then see that the scheduled transactions are consummated at those prices. For continuous market clearing, the whole process must be repeated every quarter or day or second. The scenario allows no room for orders not filled, stocks not sold, trades made at false prices. We know that those phenomena occur in reality. We know indeed that most prices—those in what Hicks called the fixprice sector in his Jahnsson lectures[12]—are set by identifiable agents and changed only at discrete intervals. We know that there are various buffers—inventories, order backlogs—for absorbing excess supply or demand at those administered prices. To describe price paths we must describe the administrators' decision-making processes.

In circumstances of complex uncertainty, we are told by students of human and organizational behavior, decision-makers generally fall back on to simple rules of thumb. They follow "satisficing" procedures rather than optimizing strategies, and stick with them until and unless outcomes worsen beyond some threshold of tolerance.[13]

---

[12] The Crisis in Keynesian Economics, op. cit.

[13] H. Simon, Administrative Behavior, 2nd ed., The Free Press, New York, 1965.

——, "A Behavioral Model of Rational Choice," Quarterly Journal of Economics, February 1955.

An example is the full-cost pricing rule common in industrial firms. The strategy may not be optimal, at least in short runs. But if all of a variety of products are so priced, then over a large range of sales environments, the firm will earn at least its target rate of return on capital. That target itself is likely to be another rule of thumb, based on estimates of normal capital costs and risks. As such it is changed to follow trends in equity and bond markets but not day-to-day fluctuations. The use of such strategies in major sectors of the economy means that their behavior differs substantially from the implications of models that assume competitive markets, continuous optimization, and daily revision of decisions in response to new information. But if we wish to model the economy we live in, should we not use whatever information we have about the way its agents actually behave?

Economic Fluctuations as Moving Equilibrium

In application to macroeconomics, the combination of rational expectations and market clearing has yielded some strong propositions. Of the two main ingredients of the new classical macroeconomics, the crucial one turns out on inspection to be the assumption of instantaneous market-clearing. There are in addition less fundamental ingredients, *ad hoc* specifications of models, which sometimes play an important role. I shall mention some of the propositions.

The most striking is the view that labor markets are always cleared, for it implies that whatever employment we

---

S. Winter, "Optimization and Evolution in the Theory of the Firm," in R. Day and T. Groves, eds., *Adaptive Economic Models*, Academic Press, New York, 1975.

have is full employment, whatever unemployment rate
exists is for the time being at least the natural rate. Contrast
Friedman's original natural rate hypothesis: Mark I
monetarism alleged that there is no inflation–unemployment trade-off available to the economy or to policymakers
in the long run. [14] It did not deny that for temporary periods,
perhaps very long in calendar time, actual unemployment
could differ from the natural rate and that policy could,
whether or not it should, exploit the difference. In Mark II
monetarism this doctrine has drifted toward denial that
there is ever any policy trade-off at all, no matter whether
the initial unemployment rate is 9% or 5% or 2%. More
precisely, there is no trade-off to systematic, anticipated
macro policy. Policy surprises may confuse market participants, and distort their expectations, thus causing markets to clear at higher or lower employment rates. Such
changes are short-lived; they last only until confusion
dissipates.

The new monetarists agree of course that employment
and unemployment fluctuate. For a variety of reasons their
current market-clearing amounts may be off trend; the
natural rate today may deviate from the permanent rate. If
so, it will move there on its own, and there is nothing that
central banks or governments can do to help. The same
propositions apply to related "markets," such as those for
the rental of services of existing capital. What appears at
times to be excess capacity is actually voluntary idleness.

As candid advocates of this position acknowledge, it is
difficult to reconcile their scenario with well established
observed facts of business cycles. If these markets are
always clearing, the sources of fluctuation must be shifting

---

[14] M. Friedman, "The Role of Monetary Policy," *American
Economic Review*, March 1968.

demand and supply curves, rather than movements away from and toward their intersection. Demand curves for labor, marginal productivity schedules, shift with technology, supply curves shift with tastes, specifically with preferences between work and leisure or other uses of time. Since intertemporal optimization is involved on both sides of the market, expectations, rational of course, about future technology and tastes are relevant too. Why should these shifts produce the smooth waves of observed cycles rather than irregular noise around steady trends? The answer of the new classical macro-economists[15] comes from outside the basic model, autoregression in the exogenous shocks of technology and taste. As an explanation of fluctuations, I submit, this is a *deus ex machina*, which only raises the further question why marginal productivities and/or disutilities of work should be auto-regressive stochastic processes. There is no *economic* business cycle theory, new or old, involved in assuming that waves in economic activity simply mirror waves in underlying technology and taste.

Thus a formidable task of the new classical macro-economists is to account for observed phenomena for which Keynesian theory has provided explanations they regard as unacceptable. The new explanations must be consistent with rational expectations and with market equilibrium, i.e., with continuous clearing of markets by prices. But in application, these principles generally require the

---

[15] R. Lucas, "Understanding Business Cycles," in K. Brunner and A. Meltzer, eds., *Stabilization of the Domestic and International Economy*, Carnegie-Rochester Conference Series on Public Policy, Vol. 5, North-Holland, Amsterdam, 1977.

——, "An Equilibrium Model of the Business Cycle," *Journal of Political Economy*, December 1975.

T. Sargent, "A Classical Macroeconomic Model for the United States," *Journal of Political Economy*, April 1976.

assistance of auxiliary *ad hoc* assumptions about the limitations of information available to agents or about the nature of random disturbances.

Consider, for example, the observation that cyclical movements of output and price, relative to their trends, are positively correlated. A Keynesian interpretation is that prices—including money wages—are sticky in the short run, throughout those large sectors of modern economies where they are set by discrete private or public administrative decisions or negotiations. As a result, economies are usually characterized by greater or smaller excess supplies of various commodities at the prevailing prices, sometimes by excess demands. Sellers and producers employ a number of quantitative buffers to handle the discrepancies; inventories, order backlogs, variation of output and employment. As aggregate demand at existing prices increases, they produce more and also raise their prices. Likewise money wages rise relative to trend as demand for labor rises and the bargaining power of unions and unorganized workers improves. This interpretation implies also that monetary and fiscal policies that add to aggregate demand will, in the short run at any rate, increase output and employment, by diminishing excess supplies at existing prices. They will also inspire some price and wage increases, as excess supplies diminish, and especially as shortages arise in increasing number of sectors. Short run price and wage Phillips curves are formalizations of this interpretation, saying that the speed at which prices and wages increase relative to trend depends inversely on the amounts of excess supply (of labor, commodity stocks, capital capacity) in the economy.

The Keynes–Phillips interpretation was subject to two waves of attack. The first was due to E. S. Phillips[16] and

---

[16] E. Phelps, "Phillips Curves, Expectations of Inflation, and Optimal Unemployment over Time," *Economica*, August 1967.

Milton Friedman.[17] They pointed out that the price *trend* is itself endogenous, so that the trade-off of unemployment for inflation is not as favorable in the long run as in the short run. In particular, if the economy is pushed into a general state of excess demand, it will take ever accelerating inflation to keep it there. But the Phelps–Friedman hypothesis did not deny either that the economy might often be in states of general excess supply or that in such states increases in aggregate demand, whether by policy or other exogenous events, could raise output and employment while also raising price levels and inflation rates. Their "natural rate" hypothesis therefore focused attention on empirical identification of the equilibrium rates of unemployment and excess capacity. The hypothesis also motivated theoretical and empirical investigations to explain why, for search and other reasons, these natural rates might be higher than Keynesian conceptions of full employment and capacity output had typically allowed. Most Keynesian economists accepted the thrust of the Phelps–Friedman analysis, even if they were not sure that the long-run Phillips curve was strictly vertical (especially for deflation) and even if they were unconvinced of the normative or equilibrium significance of states of the economy consistent with zero or stable inflation.

The second wave of attack was due to Robert Lucas,[18]

---

[17] M. Friedman, "The Role of Monetary Policy," *American Economic Review*, March 1968, elaborating his "Comment" in G. P. Schultz and R. Z. Aliber, eds., *Guidelines, Informal Controls, and the Market Place*, University of Chicago Press, Chicago, 1966.

[18] R. Lucas, "Econometric Testing of the Natural Rate Hypothesis," in O. Eckstein, ed., *The Econometrics of Price Determination*, Conference, Board of Governors of the Federal Reserve System, Washington, 1972.

and it was much more radical in its implications. It was indeed the first battle in the new classical war on Keynesian macroeconomics, and on Mark I monetarist macroeconomics for that matter. In Lucas's model, labor and product markets are always being cleared at existing wages and prices. There are no excess supplies around which can be diminished by shocks and policies that increase aggregate demand. Since the demands and supplies of rational agents depend on relative prices, e.g. on real wages, the presumption is that an increase in absolute, nominal prices will leave real quantities and relative prices unchanged in market equilibrium.

However, this classical presumption is contradicted by the evidence that short run fluctuations in output and nominal price indexes are positively correlated. Lucas's ingenious but gratuitously arbitrary solution is to postulate that the demand and supply schedules of the current period (a quarter? a year?) are based on incomplete information. Specifically, *sellers* decide how much to sell with full knowledge of the market-clearing price. Buyers, however, must decide how much to purchase in the current period before they know the market prices they will have to pay. They estimate those prices as best they can, and the quantities they purchase are their optima for the estimated prices, given their correct perception of the prices of the things they sell. Estimates of buying prices are, of course, rational expectations, formed by each agent on the basis of his correct knowledge of the structure of the economy and of the formation of government policy. This structure includes the determination of nominal prices in relation to government policies that affect the dollar volume of spending. In the absence of surprises, in these policies or other determinants of aggregate spending, the price estimates will be correct and real variables will be independent of absolute prices and of the nominal volume of spending. If there is a positive surprise in aggregate demand, however, buyers will underestimate the prices they pay. In consequence they will sell too much, and buy too much also. The reverse will occur if there is a negative surprise. As a result of these temporary surprises, real quantities will appear to be positively correlated with nominal prices and with the policy shocks that cause them to deviate from expectation. But the observed correlation does not reveal a trade-off that policymakers can systematically and repeatedly exploit. If they try to do so, private agents will incorporate the policy rules into the structure from which they estimate buying prices, and it will take deviations from the revised structure to induce deviations of output and employment from their equilibrium quantities. In any event, such deviations—based as they are on incorrect information—are distortions; the equilibrium corresponding to correct and complete information is Pareto-optimal for buyers and sellers.

Thus the Lucas model explains the same gross observations as Keynesian theory and the Phelps–Friedman hypothesis. But it has very different policy implications from both of those models. Policy can never make more than a transient difference to real outcomes, and anyway the transient difference is alway a non-optimal distortion. For Lucas, this is true regardless of the observed state of the economy, whether unemployment and excess capacity are high or low. In short, the "natural rate," at least in the sense relevant for policymakers, is whatever situation prevails. Whatever the initial condition, the policymakers can produce a lasting increase in output and employment only by an escalating sequence of unexpected inflationary shocks. It may be true, of course, that the observed state of the economy represents an equilibrium distorted downward by over-estimates of buying prices. If so, agents will rectify the situation themselves as they revise their estimates, without help from policy. Whatever the systematic policy rule, the system will move to the same real equilibrium, which might be described as the natural rate of unemployment, i.e., the rate that prevails when agents are acting on correct and complete information.

The Lucas model is very important and influential, both for its substance and for its exemplary lessons for statistical inference and for policy. Consequently it is desirable to see clearly where the conclusions come from. Of course, the twin assumptions—market-clearing and rational expectations—are essential. But so also is the *ad hoc* specification about the information available to buyers and sellers. It is this specification that enables the model to "explain" the observed correlation of nominal prices and real quantities. Suppose we reversed the positions of buyers and sellers, so that buyers know precisely what they are paying but sellers must offer supplies on the basis of predictions of the price they will get. Then the model will imply that prices and quantities are negatively correlated. A positive shock to nominal demand will raise prices, causing buyers to purchase less and sellers to offer less, both because they underestimate their selling price. Lucas's critique of Keynesian models and Phillips curves may or may not be justified. The point is that the capacity of his new macroeconomic theory to explain observations, without very questionable *ad hoc* assumptions for which no empirical evidence is offered, is exceedingly limited.[19]

The new cycle "theory" leaves many other factors unexplained. Why do people report themselves as unemployed if

---

[19] This point about the Lucas model was also made by B. Friedman in *After the Phillips Curve*, Federal Reserve Bank of Boston, 1978.

[20] H. Meyer, "Jobs and Want Ads: A Look Behind the Words," *Fortune*, November 20, 1978.

all that has happened is preference for leisure at ruling real wages? Why are voluntary quits of jobs infrequent when reported unemployment is high but frequent when it is low, while layoffs move the other way? Why are cyclical movements in and out of labor force so sensitive to vacancy and unemployment rates, so insensitive to real wages? Why, if unemployment is really voluntary and optimal search, are most searches and job changes accomplished without any interruption of employment at all? Why do vacancy rates move pro-cyclically? Why are there so few bona fide vacancies relative to willing workers?[20] Why do real wages and average labor productivity almost always move procyclically? Why do firms report utilization of capacity below preferred normal operating rates? Why, if cyclical variations of employment reflect voluntary choice, is workers' consumption so procyclical and their average propensity to consume so counter-cyclical? These and other stylized facts appear difficult to reconcile with the new classical model, but we may expect considerable ingenuity to be expended in attempts to reconcile them.

It is indeed difficult to give a rationale for the observed persistence of rising wages and prices coexistent with excess supply. It is difficult to give a convincing rationale within the paradigm of utility- and profit-maximizing behavior in competitive markets. Keynes's own observation on money wage stickiness have not satisfied the canons of proof of subsequent theorists. Increasingly their reaction has been, "If we can't explain this phenomenon to our satisfaction within the paradigm, then it doesn't happen." The difference of the new classicals from the old is, of course, that they apply the axiom to short runs, very short runs, not just to the comparative statics of equilibrium positions.

The new classical view that prices, including wages, are always market-clearing is basically the old classical equilibrium assumption that prices are flexible. As such, it has a number of familiar corollaries. One, for example, is that the real interest rate is always Wicksell's natural rate, clearing the investment/saving market. Attempts to move it by monetary policy directed at lowering or raising the nominal interest rate will fail; they will only change price levels and inflation rates. Another iron law concerns real terms of trade; they cannot be altered by devaluation c r revaluation of exchange rates, and they will be the same under floating and fixed rate regimes. The "fundamental" determinants prevail over policy every time.

Rational Expectations without Market-clearing

If the market-clearing assumption is dropped, there can be rational expectations paths along which monetary and/or fiscal policies correct a situation of under-employment. Likewise, in such situations alleged paths along which policies have no consequence frequently turn out to be generated by expectations which are not fulfilled. Consider, for example, an announced increase in the rate of monetary growth, in an economy where the money wage and price level are too high to clear the labor and capital-services markets. The alleged rational expectations path is that infla-tion expectation rises commensurately with the new monetary growth rate; nominal interest rates rise by the same amount; the real interest rate is unchanged; prices and wages start increasing as expected; output and employment are unchanged. The inconsistency is that excess supply of money has arisen as a result of the rise in nominal interest rates. Its effects on real interest and aggregate demand will defeat the assumed expectations. On the other hand, if expectations are formed to accord with a standard Keynesian–Phillips curve path, they will be realized. Increased monetary growth will lower real interest rates as expected, increasing real demand, and along the price/wage path additional supply will be available to meet the demand. Rates of price and wage inflation will rise, if at all, by less than the rise in monetary growth. Workers who spend in expectation of higher real income will earn the higher incomes. Business firms will make additional sales justifying their increases in employment and payrolls.

Likewise, rational expectations about taxes and other economic and fiscal variables are consistent with the success of fiscal measures when there is excess supply of labor and other productive factors at prevailing prices. In a Keynesian short run with under-employment, the public, even if they fully discount future taxes, can correctly calculate improvement in the present value of future real after-tax incomes. They are raised by the near-term employment of otherwise idle resources. Expecting that, households will increase their spending and make the scenario come true. Failing that, they will not have to pay additional taxes anyway, in a tax system which relates tax liabilities directly or indirectly to economic activity.

There is, in short, no expectations disappointment in these policy applications of the short-run IS-LM-Phillips curve model. What it lacks, consciously and deliberately, certainly not inadvertently, is universal continuous market-clearing.

This is not to deny that widespread public belief in monetarist dogma can generate actual expectations that make things tough for expansionary fiscal and monetary policies in situations of under-employment. It is to deny that such beliefs are rational.

It is also true that if the economy is not always in market-clearing equilibrium, rational expectations will not necessarily keep it there without the help of macro policy. Perfect foresight of price paths is generally not stabilizing, because expectations can be fulfilled along a variety of paths besides the one that returns to equilibrium. That singular path will prevail only if agents know the equilibrium and believe the system will return to it. Without belief that government policy will aim for equilibrium, agents have little reason for acting on the assumption that the equilibrium is stable.

The view that the market system possesses, for unchanging settings of government policy instruments, strong self-adjusting mechanisms that assure the stability of its full employment equilibrium is supported neither by theory nor by capitalism's long history of economic fluctuations. That government policies *can* be a source of instability is obvious; that they have in fact been destabilizing on many occasions is also undeniable. That they are the only source of shocks to an intrinsically stable mechanism is a proposition that could be seriously advanced only by persons with extravagant faith in their own abstract models and with historical amnesia. Other shocks include the changes in technology and preferences the new classicals themselves emphasize, but also changes in demographic variables, market structures, and in the public's views of those irreducibly incalculable uncertainties mentioned earlier in the lecture.

Macro policies should, to be sure, seek to stabilize expectations of the course of the economy, a task scarcely separable from that of stabilizing the actual course. This cannot be done by sticking to rules of policy that insulate it from feedbacks of information about the economy or from observations and expectations of other shocks. How it can be done, better than in the past, is a quest that continues to deserve the attention of economic theorists and econometricians. We should not be diverted from the task by the new classical macroeconomics, an intellectually ingenious construct that does not describe the societies in which we happen to live. We can take some encouragement from the

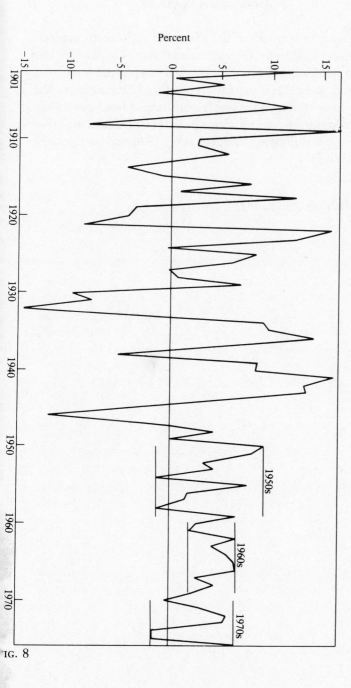

economic performance of the advanced democratic capital-
ist nations since the second world war. On this point,
Martin Baily has proved once more that a picture is worth a
thousand words. His picture, reproduced here as Figure 8,
shows how much more stable real output has been in the
United States under conscious policies of built-in and discretionary stabilization adopted since 1946 and particularly
since 1961.[21]

---

[21] M. Baily, *op. cit.*, p. 14.

III
Government Deficits and Capital Accumulation

Do government deficits absorb private saving? Does public debt diminish private demand for stocks of productive capital assets? Can the burden of current government expenditure be shifted to future generations? These are old questions. Today they are once more in the forefront of economic controversy. Few issues of economic theory and fact evoke such polar disagreement. The contesting views carry radically divergent implications for public fiscal and financial policy.

The "Ricardian" Doctrine and its Implications

Within our professional fraternity that salience of these issues today reflects in large part the powerful intellectual challenge of "the new classical macroeconomics," discussed in the previous lecture. Among its alleged implications are unqualified negative answers to the three questions at the beginning.

A dramatic summary of the position is this: the burden—or more neutrally, the effect—of government is fully measured by the size and content of real public expenditures. It is independent of how those expenditures are financed. Thus the celebrated Modigliani–Miller theorem for corporate finance is extended to government. The common thread is the downgrading of social institutions. The basic preferences of *individual* agents will prevail, with or without governments and corporations, so long as agents have the option of making transactions without the intermediation of such institutions.

The argument is simple. If government spending is not financed by current taxes, it is financed either by selling interest-bearing time obligations or by printing money. If by nonmonetary debt, the public must know that taxes will be levied in future to pay the interest, perhaps the principal too. To provide for the future taxes, households will save more, precisely enough to purchase the new government securities. Aggregate household wealth is unchanged, and so is aggregate consumption. Deferment of taxes accomplishes nothing, for good or evil. Given the present value of tax liabilities, discounted at the interest rate on government securities, the timing of the taxes makes no differences.

James Buchanan[1] calls this doctrine Ricardian, and it is true that Ricardo[2] presented the argument with characteristic clarity. However, he also added important qualifications and concluded that deferment of taxes by internal borrowing is bad fiscal policy. In spite of its inaccuracy I shall use Buchanan's terms for convenience.

---

[1] J. Buchanan, "Barro on the Ricardian Equivalence Theorem," *Journal of Political Economy*, April 1976.

[2] D. Ricardo, "On the Principles of Political Economy and Taxation," J. McCulloch, ed., *The Works of David Ricardo*, John Murray, London, pp. 146–9.

But what if monetary issue is substituted for taxation? This too will have no real effect, it is argued, but for somewhat different reasons from government debt. The new money will, and will be expected to, raise prices—enough to keep the *real* quantity of money unchanged. Alternatively, if new money is expected to be regularly issued, rational individuals will expect their cash holdings to be eroded by inflation and will save in anticipation of this tax too.

Let me remind you of some of the implications of these doctrines for macroeconomic theory and policy.

1. *The efficacy of fiscal policy in the short run.* According to conventional Keynesian theory, tax reductions and increases of transfer payments augment aggregate demand, raising employment and output or prices or both, depending on the state of the economy. Ricardian doctrine denies the potency of deficit-financed compensatory fiscal policy. Note that it does not deny the effectiveness, for good or evil, of an increase in government real expenditure. It says, however, that the effect will be the same whether the expenditure is financed by taxes or by borrowing. The so-called balanced budget multiplier applies either way. In short, supply of government securities creates its own demand. No income expansion, no multiplier process, is needed to generate the saving to buy the government deficit.

2. *The evils of government deficits.* If deficit finance is ineffectual, it is also innocuous. It does not "crowd out" private capital formation or foreign investment. Nor can timid or profligate legislatures and ministers be blamed for inflation, so long as they are willing to finance their deficits by interest-bearing bonds rather than by printing money. This is why the Ricardian view is as unpalatable to fiscal conservatives like Buchanan as to Keynesians.

3. *The long run burden of public debt*. Fiscal conservatives, including politicians and laymen as well as economists, have long argued that debt finance irresponsibly burdens future generations for current government programs. In the long standing debate on internal public debt,[3] some economists have argued that the burden of diverting resources to public use, the value of the contemporary private uses foregone, cannot be shifted in time. Others have pointed out that future generations can be burdened to the extent that deficit finance diminishes the stocks of human and nonhuman capital they inherit.[4] The revived Ricardian doctrine says, however, that this will not happen, that capital stock will not be crowded out by government debt.

Note the parallelism of short and long run. Keynesians believe that expansionary fiscal policy works in situations of underemployment because deficits absorb saving which, in the absence of sufficient private investment demand, would vanish via contraction of income. By the same token, they believe that in long run full employment states public debt satisfies some demand for wealth and displaces some capital. Ricardians believe that deficit spending is futile in the short run and innocuous in the long run.

4. *The Pigou effect*. In the first lecture I revisited the "real balance" effect and recalled the controversy about the proper base for its calculations. Does the base include all public debt or only monetary issue or nothing? The Ricardian position would be that a permanent reduction in the

---

[3] Summarized in J. Ferguson, ed., *Public Debt and Future Generations*, University of North Carolina Press, Chapel Hill, 1964.

[4] For example, F. Modigliani, "Long-run Implications of Alternative Fiscal Policies and the Burden of the National Debt," *Economic Journal*, December 1961.

price level increases equally the real value of the government's non-monetary obligations and the real value of the associated tax liabilities. The "Keynesian" view would support the Pigou effect, reckoning a greater consumption stimulus for the government's creditors than consumption deterrent to future taxpayers.

5. *The effects of open market operations.* Central bank purchases of government securities extinguish both the stream of interest payments to the public and the associated future taxes. From the Ricardian viewpoint, the transaction increases household wealth by the full amount. It is no different in effect from money creation to finance government outlays, or from that textbook favorite, "money rain." In either case, a monetarist Ricardian might believe that the price level would adjust to keep the real quantity of money unchanged. Note also that, from the same Ricardian viewpoint, a "bond rain" would have no effect. Thus the Ricardian equivalence theorem is fundamental, perhaps indispensable, to monetarism.

The Keynesian view would downgrade the wealth gain and consumption stimulus attributable to the expected reduction in future tax liabilities. Therefore an increment of money stock arising from open market transactions would be regarded as less expansionary or inflationary than the same amount arising from deficit finance or "money rain."

6. *Social security.* Social insurance for retirement, death, and disability is one form of public debt. By compulsory contributions, whether by employee or employer, during working life, citizens build up an immense, if not precise, total of claims on government. Some critics in the United States have estimated and deplored the displacement of productive capital investment which they allege this vast

accumulation of claims represents.[5] But, of course, the Ricardian calculation tells us that those benefits stimulate consumption no more than the associated stream of anticipated social insurance taxes deters it. Indeed pay-as-you-go financing of social security, as in the United States, cannot in principle yield the participants on average more than the growth rate of the system. As this is less than the rate of return on private investment, rational participants could regard the forced diversion of saving as a net loss.

Critique of Ricardian Doctrine as Restated by Barro

The so-called Ricardian argument has recently been forcefully restated and elaborated in an influential article by Robert Barro, one of the new classical macro-economists.[6] I wish to consider his argument in some detail.

1. *Life cycles and bequests*. If consumers' horizons do not extend beyond their own lifetimes, if they are indifferent to the living standards of their surviving children, deferment of taxes to the next generation will clearly raise consumption by the current generation. Just as James Buchanan

---

[5] M. Feldstein, "Social Security, Induced Retirement, and Aggregate Capital Accumulation," *Journal of Political Economy* September/October 1974.

[6] R. Barro, "Are Government Bonds Net Wealth?", *Journal of Political Economy*, November/December 1974.

Barro is not and does not claim to be the first modern re-discoverer of the Ricardian equivalence theorem. He cites: J. Tobin, "Asset Holdings and Spending Decisions," *American Economic Review Papers and Proceedings*, May 1952.

M. J. Bailey, *National Income and the Price Level*, McGraw-Hill, New York, 1962, pp. 75–7.

fears, public debt issue permits the generation in power to shift tax burdens to generations without political voice. At the other extreme, for consumers with infinite horizons, the intertemporal budget constraint is independent of the timing of taxes. Anyway this is true if the government bonds bear the same interest rate at which consumers can make intertemporal shifts of consumption. Consequently the optimal consumption/saving plan will not be changed by substituting debt finance for current taxation.

Barro's contribution is to show how mortal households can have effectively infinite horizons. The condition is that each generation include in its utility function, along with consumption at various stages of its lifetime, the *utility* of the next generation. The child's utility is a function—in indirect form—of his endowment plus the bequest received from the parent. Within a given present value of taxation, a shift in timing from one generation to the next leaves the parent facing the same budget constraint as before. He will make up for the heavier taxation in store for the child by providing a larger bequest. The chain of overlapping generations behaving in this manner makes the horizon of each generation effectively infinite.

This ingenious construction invites several comments:

a   The chain is broken if any generation is childless or is indifferent to the utility of its successor. Expecting this in advance, the current generation has incentive to increase its own consumption if taxes are deferred beyond the break in the chain.

b   As everybody knows, some households in each generation are childless, or indifferent to the lots of their own children. These households will consume more if their taxes are lightened at the expense of later generations. The remaining households, who have children and care about them, then perceive that their descendants will bear not only the taxes they are spared but the taxes their

childless or indifferent contemporaries are spared.
These parents cannot maintain both their lifetime consumption and the utility of their children; general
deferment of taxes lightens their budget constraint.
They will give way on both margins; they will increase
their bequests but not by enough to pay their children's
taxes. Taking both kinds of households together, debt
finance increases current consumption.

c   Parents' utility may well depend in some degree on the
size of their bequests to their children, independently of
the utility or total endowment of the children. Giving is
frequently, perhaps usually, for the gratification of the
giver, not just the welfare of the receiver. If so, bequests
are related to the wealth of the parents as well as, or
more than, to the expected needs of the heirs. Equal
division among several children, regardless of differences among them in other endowments, is after all a
customary pattern. The thrust of this observation is
that bequests will not be increased enough to keep
heirs' utility intact when taxes are shifted on to the
heirs.

d   Here is a third way in which the infinite chain may be
broken. Many households, even those concerned with
children's utility, will find utility optima at zero-
bequest corners rather than at interior points. They
would prefer negative bequests, but these are not
within their options. Such families will of course
bequeath no more but consume more if their taxes are
reduced and those of their heirs correspondingly
increased. Corner solutions are likely when households' utility functions place small weight on the future
utility of their heirs, or place large probability weight
on the possibility that the chain will somehow be
broken. Corner solutions are more likely too in progressive economies where parents can normally expect

their children and grandchildren to be much better off than they are.

2. *Liquidity constraints.* Even within the lifetime of one generation, households are generally not able to shift consumption at will from a later date to an earlier date. When such intertemporal substitution is possible, it can usually be achieved only at a higher rate of interest than can be earned on saving. Even in countries with sophisticated financial institutions and well-developed capital markets, opportunities for borrowing against future earnings from labor are limited. Compulsory or contractual saving, down payment and collateral requirements, illiquidity of future retirement pensions—these and other "imperfections" —further limit the intertemporal fungibility of lifetime resources, not to mention intergenerational resources.

There are good reasons for all these departures from the theorist's presumptive norm of perfect capital markets, but they are outside my current topic. The implication of these facts of life is that a large fraction of households, even in affluent societies, are liquidity-constrained as well as wealth-constrained. Their horizons for consumption plans are shorter than their lifetimes, let alone the lifetimes of their lineal families. They will not be indifferent to the opportunity to defer tax payments. Even if they themselves must pay the taxes later, they will increase their consumption now. In effect the government lends to them at its borrowing rate of interest, an option not otherwise available in the credit market.

Liquidity constraints also, incidentally, weaken the force of the argument that unfunded social insurance diminishes the total saving of life-cycle consumers. The fear is that taxes to pay for higher benefits will not reduce private consumption but will be used for government consumption. It is not fully justified, to the extent that liquidity-constrained workers cannot avoid reducing consumption when their compulsory social insurance contributions are increased. Here the liquidity constraints prevent households from undoing the government's attempt to defer their consumption until they retire. Moreover, some households will, as Barro argues, increase their bequests or gifts to heirs rather than their own lifetime consumption, partially if not wholly alleviating the higher taxes their children must pay to support their parents' retirement insurance benefits. For a combination of reasons, therefore, Feldstein and others are probably overstating their case that pay-as-you-go social security diminishes capital formation.[7]

3. *Non-lump-sum taxes.* So far I have adhered to Barro's assumption of lump-sum taxes, and I have advanced several reasons why consumption/saving plans are not neutral with respect to timing of tax payments. The bias is invariably in one direction: compared to current taxation, debt finance of government expenditure increases current consumption, reduces the saving available to purchase assets other than government securities. These conclusions are reinforced if real-world taxes are considered in place of lump-sum taxes.

There are two senses in which the nature of the tax system is relevant. First, if tax liabilities are not specified amounts levied on named individuals but amounts related to individuals' circumstances—income, wealth, consumption, family size, etc.—then anticipated taxes depend on expectations of those circumstances and of tax legislation. Second, of course, non-lump-sum levies generally induce tax-reducing behavior.

---

[7] J. Tobin, "Discussion," in *Funding Pensions: Issues and Implications for Financial Markets*, Federal Reserve Bank of Boston, 1976.

To take up the second point first, taxation of wealth or income from wealth makes a gaping hole in the "Ricardian" case, as Ricardo himself well knew. This is most obvious if current lump-sum transfer payments or per capita tax credits are financed by debt issues to be serviced, at least in part, by future wealth taxes. Few of us would doubt that the combination induces some substitution against saving and capital formation. This will be true even if consumers are immortal, or, via the Barro inter-generational linkage, have effectively infinite horizons. The same qualitative effect will occur if future wealth taxation is substituted for current wealth taxation, for the reduction in current taxes does not help future accumulation. If the change in timing had been anticipated, the net results over time and generations are not clear, but there will be a bulge in consumption for the favored generations.

What about wage taxes? To the extent that they tax proceeds of human capital investments, the above remarks apply. They may also induce substitution in favor of leisure and other uses of time that escape the scrutiny of tax collectors. Anticipating such substitutions by his heirs, a Barro model parent will know that to maintain her heirs' utilities, it is unnecessary to maintain their endowments against expected increases in wage taxes. Substitutions will do part of the job, so the parent may in good conscience consume herself some of the fruits of her tax reductions.

The first point is important even if tax-reducing substitutions are negligible. The reason is that tax liabilities, individual and aggregate, are at least as uncertain as the tax bases on which they depend.

a   The Barro model parent is, of course, not really certain of her heir's income-earning capacity. The function of bequest is not just to raise the heir's expected utility. It is also to guard against disappointment or disaster in the heir's earning power. A parent so minded will provide a higher bequest the larger her estimate of the variance of the child's endowment. Taxation of income, wealth, or consumption lowers that variance. Suppose, then, that the expectation of higher taxes for debt service focuses on higher tax *rates*. The increase in the mean expected tax burden on the heir will tend to raise the parent's bequest; but given her uncertainty about the heir's other pre-tax endowments, reduction in their after-tax variance tends to diminish bequests.

b   Essentially the same point can be made without resort to the inter-generational model. Suppose the government gives a worker one week's extra wages today while suggesting that he will pay extra taxes of about two weeks' wages in about ten years. However, today's bonus takes the form of a bond to pay him consumption value in ten years. If he accepts he will feel wealthier, i.e., his future consumption is more secure. He will therefore consume more now. The bond makes up for the mean decline in his future after-tax income. Since the bond is sure, the uncertainty of future consumption is reduced. Its variance is further reduced by the increase in tax rate. In addition the bond has a liquidity advantage. It will meet interim consumption in emergencies more surely and cheaply than borrowing against future wage income.

Keynesians have always argued that the discount rate for future taxes is the one appropriate for the streams of income on which the taxes are levied;[8] given the uncertainties in those streams, that rate is higher than the discount for government obligations. The differential means that gov-

---

[8] W. Smith, "A Neo-Keynesian View of Monetary Policy," in *Controlling Monetary Aggregates*, Federal Reserve Bank of Boston, 1969.

ernment bond issue does indeed raise net wealth even if taxpayers correctly expect that taxes will be increased to service the added debt.

The above argument has been stated for consumption-indexed bonds, but it applies also to currency-denominated bonds. They do not provide the same security, but they do hedge the taxes levied to service the debt itself. Uncertainties about inflation make currency and promises to pay currency less attractive relative to real assets. Narrowing of the related discount differentials means that the gain in wealth due to debt finance is smaller when inflation prospects are more uncertain.

4. *Deficits and short-run stabilization policy*. So far my discussion of the effects of debt finance has concerned only long-run equilibrium, with full employment. So far my argument supports the view that debt finance does, in some degree, crowd out capital stock, a view shared by Keynesians and by conservative theorists like Buchanan. The same argument, I observed earlier, suggests that Keynesian fiscal policy will work in the short run. That is, substitution of debt issue for current taxation will stimulate current consumption; in conditions of under-employment, the resulting expansion of aggregate real demand will increase output and employment.

All the points previously advanced apply in the short-run context, and they are reinforced by a powerful additional mechanism. If resources are unemployed for lack of demand, their re-employment will augment the stream of actual and expected household incomes. The present value of the stream will be raised *even* if households expect eventually to service the additional debt from taxes on their incomes. The Keynesian scenario is entirely consistent with rational expectations.

Is this also true of the Ricardian scenario? The answer is

no, if taxes are in fact geared to incomes and are correctly perceived. For suppose that households fail to spend any of their transfers or tax reductions, instead buying government bonds to provide for expected future taxes. Incomes do not increase; deficits continue; public debt, household bond holdings, and expected future taxes grow. But the expectations of higher taxes are never confirmed.

We can imagine fiscal policies and associated expectations under which both Ricardian and Keynesian scenarios are self-consistent. This is not surprising. "Rational expectations" paths are generally not unique when the system is not in equilibrium. If annual budget balance were the objective of fiscal policy, as in the days of the British "Treasury View," shared by President Herbert Hoover and the last Weimar Chancellor, Heinrich Bruening, the appearance of a deficit during cyclical recession would lead to expectations of higher taxes and accelerate the recession. If full employment budget balance is the understood objective, tax increases will not be expected during recessions and periods of under-employment. Then tax expectations and related expenditure decisions will support the understood countercyclical policy. Baily[9] shows that this may well have happened in the United States after the second world war, especially in the 1960s.

In the previous lecture I discussed the more fundamental contentions of the new classical macroeconomics, that under-employment disequilibria can never occur, that aggregate demand can never be deficient, that prices and money wages continuously clear product and labor markets, that systematic fiscal and monetary demand management can never alter these equilibria. In this lecture I simply

---

[9] M. N. Baily, "Stabilization Policy and Private Economic Behavior," *Brookings Papers on Economic Activity*, 1:1978.

argue that those strong contentions gain no credibility from the Ricardian strictures about fiscal policy.

Statistical Evidence Recently Offered in Support of Ricardian Doctrine

I cannot attempt in this lecture a thorough discussion of the statistical or econometric evidence for the Ricardian equivalence theorem or for the opposing Keynesian position. The relevant literature is enormous. It includes all the competing estimates of the effects of fiscal and monetary policies, in large scale structural models and in single reduced form equations. You are all familiar with this long and continuing empirical controversy. I will simply observe that almost all macro-econometric models for the United States economy continue to show significant multipliers for tax reductions or increases in transfer payments financed by non-monetary debt issue. They imply that such debt issues do absorb private saving. The St. Louis model is an exception in assigning no lasting overall expansionary power to pure fiscal policy, even to exhaustive expenditure. But that model does not support Ricardian doctrine either. The mechanism that nullifies fiscal expansion could be crowding out of private investment by higher interest rates. Under the Ricardian scenario, extra saving to pay future taxes would do the job without any rise of interest rates.

I shall confine myself to a brief comment on some recent calculations inspired by the Ricardian thesis. The most direct attempt is that of Kochin.[10] Encouraged by observing that high personal saving ratios occurred in 1970–1 coincident

---

[10] L. Kochin, "Are Future Taxes Anticipated by Consumers?", *Journal of Money, Credit, and Banking*, August 1974.

with record federal deficits, he introduced the deficit as a second explanatory variable in annual time series regression of personal consumption on disposable income (i.e., after-tax personal income) 1952–71. He found negative coefficients for the deficit, two to three times their standard errors. Kochin regarded these findings as confirming the view that consumers rationally save in anticipation of future taxes (either explicit taxes or inflation "taxes" on money balances).

His conceptual and statistical procedures are subject to a number of questions, but for two reasons it is unnecessary to go into them for the purposes of this lecture. First, the coefficients of deficit in his preferred regressions are only one fourth the absolute size of the marginal propensity to consume from disposable income. His equations imply, therefore, that a dollar increase in both disposable income and deficit by tax reduction or transfer payment would be a big stimulus to consumption. Second, the casually observed coincidence that inspired Kochin's regression calculations was reversed after 1971. In the subsequent five years deficits soared to new records, while personal saving rates were unusually *low*. Statistically, the result of adding the years 1972–6 in calculating Kochin's regression is to deprive the federal deficit of all explanatory power.[11]

David and Scadding[12] also examine household saving behavior and conclude that deficit spending will not absorb saving in the short or long run. However, their argument is

---

[11] W. Buiter and J. Tobin, "Debt Neutrality: A Brief Review of Doctrine and Evidence," unpublished, to appear in G. von Furstenberg, ed., *Social Security versus Private Saving in Post-industrial Societies*, American Council of Life Insurance, 1979.

[12] P. David and J. Scadding, "Private Savings: Ultra-rationality, Aggregation and 'Denison's Law'," *Journal of Political Economy*, March/April 1974.

quite different from the Ricardian equivalence theorem that inspired Kochin's regressions. Their point of departure is "Denison's Law," the observed long run constancy of the Gross Private Saving Rate (GPSR), the ratio of private saving, households and businesses combined, to GNP in the United States. Their explanation is "ultra-rationality"—households internalize the actions of the businesses they own, incorporated and unincorporated, and adjust their own saving to offset dollar for dollar changes in business saving. In short, they extend the Modigliani–Miller theorem beyond finance to accumulation.

Whatever the theoretical and empirical merits of this proposition—actually, GPSR appears to have slipped by one point since the second world war—it does not imply public debt neutrality. Rather, it implies that a reduction of taxes (net of transfers) increases consumption dollar for dollar. So "ultra-rationality" à la David and Scadding clearly implies not that personal saving adjusts to compensate for government deficits but precisely the opposite. Disturbed by this implication, which seems to imply that consumers internalize business behavior but not government actions, the authors propose a way out. Their ultra-rational households, they decide, must regard taxes as financing collective consumption, perfectly equivalent to private consumption, and deficits as financing public investment, 100% substitutable for private capital formation. On this basis they conclude that "an extra dollar of government deficit will displace a dollar of private *investment* expenditure" (my italics), a completely gratuitous conclusion unsupported by their empirical study of private saving behavior. It is especially absurd to apply it to short run variations of deficit due either to automatic cyclical variation in revenues and transfers or to discretionary stabilization policies. These do not change the mix of government expenditure between consumption and investment;

and no consumer-taxpayers, wherever they fall on the spectrum of rationality, would think they did. Yet David and Scadding, and many who cite their article, evidently believe they have dealt a devastating blow to the use of fiscal policy as an instrument of stabilization.

Taylor, using U.S. quarterly data 1953–69, finds that the marginal propensities to consume from tax reductions, especially social insurance contributions, and from transfer payments are extraordinarily low relative to those from changes in pre-tax earnings.[13] While his results cast doubt on the effectiveness of tax and transfer changes as instruments of stabilization, they do not support the debt neutrality hypothesis. They are more consistent with the life cycle or permanent income saving models, which imply that temporary fiscal measures are weaker than permanent changes of income. Taylor's results also are consistent with the criticisms of unfunded retirement insurance. In any event, the cyclical multi-collinearity of taxes, transfers, deficits, and pre-tax incomes makes it very difficult to estimate their separate effects on household consumption and saving. Statistically it is hard to improve on the simple short-run relationship of consumption to disposable income.[14]

Steady-state Effects of Fiscal Policy: Sketch of a Model

I hope that my review of the theoretical and empirical debate has convinced you that government finance cannot be simply swept aside and ignored as irrelevant to real

---

[13] L. Taylor, "Saving Out of Different Types of Income," *Brookings Papers on Economic Activity*, 2:1971.

[14] For further review of evidence, see W. Buiter and J. Tobin, *op. cit.*

economic outcomes. In conclusion, I would like to sketch a model of the long-run consequences of alternative financing policies for capital formation and inflation. In other papers[15] similar models are presented in much more detail and their short-run and long-run properties are examined.

The main point I would emphasize here is the following: Deficit financing may cause inflation, or it may crowd out capital formation. But it is unlikely to do both. In the degree it is inflationary, it makes money a less attractive asset and encourages saving in other forms, including productive capital. Under fiscal policies where deficits are a larger share of national income, the actual and expected erosion of stocks of money and nominal debt by inflation makes them smaller fractions of national wealth. The "inflation tax" is not a lump-sum tax, and substitution to avoid it is sufficient reason that money-financed deficits are not neutral. It may seem paradoxical, but it is not really surprising, that larger nominal stocks may turn out to be smaller real stocks, not only relatively but absolutely. In the long run, real stocks must accord with public asset demands; the price level and inflation rate adjust government-issued supplies to those demands.

On the other hand, it is conceivable that deficit financing will be counter-inflationary, in the sense that steady states corresponding to fiscal policies with higher deficits show lower inflation rates. They will also have higher real interest

---

[15] J. Tobin and W. Buiter, "Fiscal and Monetary Policies, Capital Formation, and Economic Activity," unpublished, to appear in G. von Furstenberg, ed., *The Government and Capital Formation*, American Council of Life Insurance, 1979.
J. Tobin, "Deficit Spending and Crowding Out in Shorter and Longer Runs," H. I. Greenfield, *et al.*, eds., *Economic Theory for Economic Efficiency: Essays in Honor of Abba P. Lerner*, M.I.T. Press, Cambridge, 1979.

rates and lower capital stocks. But stability is dubious for steady-state solutions of these configurations.

The model I have in mind describes fiscal policy by three parameters: the fraction e of net national product purchased by government; the fraction t collected in taxes net of transfers; the fraction γ of the government deficit financed by issue of base money. The remaining fraction $1-\gamma$ is financed by issue of interest-bearing obligations, which for convenience I take to be consols bearing a coupon of $1 per year, free of tax. The real rate of return on money is $-i$, the negative of the inflation rate. The real rate on bonds, market-determined, is r_B. The market value of bonds is $1/(r_B+i)$, the reciprocal of their nominal rate of return. The real interest cost of new debt (in both forms money and consols) r_d is a weighted average of the two real rates, $r_B(1-\gamma) + (-i)\gamma$. In a steady state, with γ constant over time, this is also the real interest cost of existing debt. If d is the ratio of total debt to national product, then the government budget identity can be written as:

$$(1) \qquad e - t = (g-r_d)d = (g-r_B(1-\gamma) + i\gamma)d,$$

where g is the natural growth rate of the economy.

Wealth-owners also can hold capital bearing a real rate r_K. In steady state equilibrium the aggregate capital/output ratio is inversely related to this rate by $k(r_K)$. I write the steady-state demands for the three assets, relative to aggregate income, as functions $f^J(r_K(1-t), r_B, -i, t)$, $(J = K, B, M)$, i.e., as functions of the three after-tax rates of return and of the tax rate. These must equal the steady-state asset supplies:

$$(2) \qquad f^K(\overset{+}{r_K(1}-t), \overset{-}{r_B,} \overset{-}{-i}, \overset{-}{t}) \qquad = k(r_K)$$

$$(3) \qquad f^B(\overset{-}{r_K(1}-t), \overset{+}{r_B,} \overset{-}{-i}, \overset{-}{t}) \qquad = (1-\gamma)\frac{e-t}{g-r_d}$$

(4) $\qquad f^M(\overset{-}{r_K(1-t)},\ \overset{-}{r_B},\ \overset{+}{-i},\ \overset{-}{t}) \qquad = \gamma\dfrac{e-t}{g-r_d}$

The sum of these three equations gives the wealth/income ratio:

(5) $\qquad f(\overset{+}{r_K(1-t)},\ \overset{+}{r_B},\ \overset{+}{-i},\ \overset{-}{t}) = k+d$

Equation (5) is the stock equivalent of the "IS" curve, which says that private savings equals capital investment plus the government deficit.

The signs above the arguments in the functions of equations (2)–(5) indicate the assumed impacts. The interest rate effects are taken to be consistent with gross substitutability among the assets, with the own effects dominant. That is, an increase in an interest rate may induce additional saving, but only in the asset whose rate has increased. Taxes, apart from their effect on the after-tax return to capital, are assumed to deter all forms of asset accumulation.

The system (2), (3), (4)—plus the definition of r_d given above—determines the three rates (r_K, r_B, $-i$) as functions of the policy parameters (e, t, γ). Note that in any steady state resources are fully employed and expectations are automatically rational. Expected and actual values of variables coincide and are constant. The question of this lecture is the effect of t on the steady-state profit rate r_K and thus on the capital intensity $k(r_K)$. The debt neutrality proposition is that variation of t has no effect.

For the neutrality proposition to hold, the tax rate t must not enter f^K, the left hand side of (2), either directly or indirectly. This requires several special and implausible assumptions:

a   Taxes do not affect the after-tax return on capital. As I have observed several times in the lecture, the neutrality doctrine assumes lump-sum taxes and ignores substitution effects.

b   Taxes do not affect saving and asset demands in other
    ways, e.g. by altering lifetime labor income or by alter-
    ing the bite of liquidity constraints. As I have observed,
    the neutrality doctrine assumes infinite horizons.
c   Demand for capital stock is independent of the yields of
    alternative assets, here money and bonds.

If those partial derivatives of f^K are not zero, then changes in
t will affect the demand for capital indirectly. In equations
(3) and (4), t necessarily affects asset supplies on the right
hand side, even if assumptions (a) and (b) are used to eliminate t from asset demands on the left. Reduction of t
increases debt (assuming g exceeds r_d) and alters, probably
lowers, r_B and $-i$. Unless those rates are irrelevant to the
demand for capital f^K, both r_K and $k(r_K)$ are bound to vary
with t. From this perspective, the Barro argument and its
counterpart for the "inflation tax" on money may be seen as
elaborate rationalization of the view that government-
issued financial assets are not substitutes, even imperfect
substitutes, for real capital.

I will not provide a formal analysis of this model here.[16]
With the help of Figure 9 we can see what is going on. The
price of using a two-dimensional diagram for a
3-dimensional model is that we relegate to the second order
any changes in the relative rates of return on the two types
of debt, money and bonds. We keep the composition of the
debt unchanged. The horizontal axis measures the compo-
site r_d; leftward from the vertical line at $r_d = g$, the same axis
measures $g - r_d$. The vertical axis measures d, the ratio of
public debt to income, $d + k$, the ratio of wealth to income,
and their difference k, the capital/output ratio. The curve

---

[16] See, however, J. Tobin, "Deficit Spending and Crowding Out
    in Shorter and Longer Runs," and J. Tobin and W. Buiter,
    "Fiscal and Monetary Policies, Capital Formation, and
    Economic Activity," both cited above.

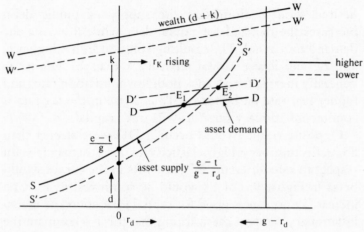

FIG. 9

WW indicates that desired wealth f is an increasing function of r_d, given r_K and other variables. Curve SS represents the supply of public debt, $(e-t)/(g-r_d)$, as a function of r_d. It is a rectangular hyperbola, asymptotic to the horizontal axis and to the vertical line at $r_d = g$, crossing the vertical axis at $(e-t)/g$. In the relevant range, movement up SS leaves less (vertical) room for capital k in total wealth WW. This means that movement up SS brings an increase in r_K.

Curve DD represents portfolio balance, as between public debt of the prescribed composition $(\gamma, 1-\gamma)$ and capital. It shows d and k desired at each value of r_d, assuming the r_K which would be consistent with the *supply* of public debt, i.e., the difference between WW and SS, at that r_d. Curve DD may or may not be steeper than SS. In Figure 9 it is less steep. Point E_1 is an equilibrium. To its right there is excess supply of debt, excess demand for capital; to its left the reverse.

The dashed curves W'W', S'S', D'D' illustrate shifts associated with a higher value of t. Greater taxation lowers desired wealth, diminishes the supply of public debt, increases the demand for public debt while lowering the demand for capital. The resulting solution E_2 has higher r_d and r_K, and lower capital intensity k than E_1. Higher r_d generally means, for given γ, both lower inflation rate i and higher real rate on bonds r_B. Thus a rise in the tax rate is counter-inflationary but "crowds out" capital.

Opposite results would occur if DD were steeper than SS, reflecting very high elasticity of asset demands with respect to rate differentials. The shifts in the curves would be as in Figure 9; but E_2 would be southwest of E_1. The increase in tax rate is good for capital formation and is also inflationary. I repeat the warning that this is a comparative statics exercise. The steady state equilibria being compared may not be stable.

In conclusion, I express the view that answers to the important questions with which I began are not to be found in appeals to first principles that allegedly support sweeping theorems of equivalence and neutrality. Rather they are to be sought in empirical studies of asset choice and saving behavior. I hope that theoretical constructions of the type I have illustrated in my concluding section, further discussed in the next lecture, offer some help in the formulation of those empirical studies.

IV
Portfolio Choice and Asset Accumulation

The common theme of these lectures is how theorists do and should model the macroeconomic structures they are trying to describe. In this final lecture my focus will be on the modeling of stocks and flows, and thus inevitably on the treatment of time. I shall be particularly concerned with the Keynesian model and the famous IS/LM formalization of it by Sir John Hicks, [1] the principal analytic apparatus in many macro textbooks, courses, journal articles, policy applications throughout the world. I shall consider critically its possible interpretations, some objections to them raised by others, and some of my own. Yet I want to begin by saying that I do not think the apparatus is discredited. I still believe that, carefully used and taught, it is a powerful instrument for understanding our economies and the impacts of policies upon them.

---

[1] J. Hicks, "Mr. Keynes and the Classics: A Suggested Interpretation," *Econometrica*, April 1937.

The lecture will be in two parts, the first devoted to general methodological discussion, the second to some specific suggestions on macro modelbuilding with illustrations of their application.

The Keynesian Short-run Model and its Interpretation

In my introductory remarks before the first lecture I referred to charges that standard macro models neglect "the government budget constraint" and therefore come to incorrect conclusions on the effects of fiscal policy. True enough, no equation for the government budget appears in a standard IS/LM model; whether its omission is a source of error is another question. With respect to modeling methodology, the issue is much broader.

A Hicksian IS/LM model is a set of simultaneous equations. What is their solution supposed to represent? Is it an equilibrium in real time, with the endogenous variables remaining stationary in value until the system is shocked by changes in exogenous variables? If so, we may analyze the stability of the equilibrium, as Hicks himself has done.[2]

However, we know that the IS/LM solution cannot generally be a stationary equilibrium. The values that the solution gives to the flow variables in the model usually imply that stocks are increasing or decreasing. Thus net investment may be positive, so that the capital stock is increasing. Savings may be positive, so that household net worth is increasing. Yes, the government deficit may be positive, so that public debt, in some form monetary or non-monetary, is increasing. These stock changes matter because the stocks

---

[2] J. R. Hicks, *A Contribution to the Theory of the Trade Cycle*, Clarendon Press, Oxford, 1950, Chapters XI and XII.

are, or should be, arguments in the functions determining the flows: for example, capital in the investment and production functions, wealth in the saving function. As a result of these internal dynamics, the IS/LM solution is generally changing as time passes, even though no exogenous shocks are occurring. The only stationary solutions, if any exist, are those which imply stationary stocks—or the balanced growth equivalent, stocks all growing at a common proportional rate.

Keynes was well aware that the model of the *General Theory* described only a temporary short-run equilibrium. He excused the failure to track changes in capital stock and their effects, referring to "factors in which the changes seem to be so slow . . . as to have only a small and comparatively negligible short-term influence on . . . our present object [which] is to discover what determines at any time the national income of a given economic system. . . ."[3]

Though Keynes was not explicit about assets other than capital, the spirit of the approach is presumably the same: the time span for which the model is intended is too short for flows to make noticeable changes in stocks. With respect to government deficit and debt, this might or might not be true. A budget deficit of $50 billion per year increases a $500 billion debt by only 10% in a year, but it would increase a $50 billion debt by 100%.

However, the standard IS/LM model pays no particular attention to non-monetary public debt as such. It amalgamates government securities with all other non-monetary assets as the undifferentiated second store of wealth to which "the" rate of interest applies. Any *per annum* government deficit will alter this total quite slowly. If this aggregation is accepted, then the relevant stock changes are

---

[3] *General Theory*, p. 247.

those of money and of this second asset, which together sum to private wealth. Growth of non-monetary public debt is just one form of growth in non-monetary wealth. The relevant questions are what effects this growth has on consumption and on demand for money. The same questions arise with respect to saving that finances private investment rather than government deficit. Keynes's pragmatic answer would still apply—flows change the stocks so slowly that neglect of stock changes does no violence.

But if government securities are regarded as imperfect portfolio substitutes for private debts and for equities in physical capital, the comprehensive second asset implicit in simple IS/LM models should be broken down into two or more constituents and "the" interest rate replaced by a vector of two or more interest rates. Then it would be important to track separately the growth of these differentiated asset stocks, the more important the less substitutable they are in the portfolios of wealth-owners.

There are other contexts where failure to keep track of the effects of flows on stocks could be misleading, where interpretation of the solution of an IS/LM type model as an equilibrium stationary for any interesting period of time would miss important effects. Consider, for example, the well-known Mundell–Fleming extension of the Hicksian apparatus to a "small" open economy with capital mobility. [4] The IS/LM solution is governed by the foreign interest rate, exogenous to the home economy. With a fixed exchange rate the IS curve determines domestic income and

---

[4] R. Mundell, "Capital Mobility and Stabilization Policy Under Fixed and Flexible Exchange Rates," *Canadian Journal of Economics and Political Science*, November 1963.

J. Fleming, "Domestic Financial Policies Under Fixed and Under Floating Exchange Rates," *IMF Staff Papers*, November 1962.

a trade balance not necessarily zero. Consequently the net foreign assets of the economy, whether held privately or officially, are changing. The model does not, however, trace the consequences of these stock changes, which may build up to quite a large proportion of initial stocks in a short time. Under flexible rates too the equilibrium trade balance is in general non-zero; income is determined in the money equation, domestic absorption by income and the foreign interest rate, and their difference is the trade balance. Both the exchange rate and the foreign asset flows, all on private account in this regime, adjust to the trade balance thus determined. The stock consequences of these flows are not modeled. However, the neat and powerful conclusions of the model regarding effectiveness of monetary and fiscal policies under the two exchange regimes do not survive explicit tracking of foreign asset stocks.[5]

A rigorous way to interpret Keynes's procedure and Hicks's formalization of the model is to regard the IS/LM solution as the values of the variables at a point in time. Then the model is a slice, in time of measure zero, of a continuous-time dynamic model. Asset stocks are among the state variables of the system at that time; they are constant, i.e., independent of the solution, insofar as they are inherited from the past. They change as time passes, and their changes move the instantaneous IS and LM curves. The "short run" model has a new solution each microsecond; whether, when, where it settles down requires dynamic analysis.[6]

---

[5] J. Tobin and J. B. de Macedo, "The Short-Run Macroeconomics of Floating Exchange Rates: An Exposition," J. Chipman and C. Kindleberger, eds., *Flexible Exchange Rates and the Balance of Payments: Essays in Memory of Egon Sohmen*, forthcoming.
[6] An example of this type of model is:
J. Tobin and W. Buiter, "Long Run Effects of Fiscal and

Under this interpretation, it is still possible to answer certain questions by comparative static analysis of the temporary solution. For example, how will the momentary solution be different if, for given values of stocks and other state variables, government expenditure or taxes or transfer payments are different? For this question, the stock effects of the financing of the government deficit or surplus are irrelevant. However the deficit is being financed, however large the deficit is, the stocks of money and non-monetary debt cannot change by finite amounts during an infinitesimally small interval of time. You may be driving on the highway at 50 km/hr or at 150 km/hr, but in either case you cover zero distance in zero time. Of course it really is no answer either to highway policemen or to those who are worried about the eventual consequences of deficit spending to refer them to the later but often unwritten chapters on dynamics.

As for monetary policy, it is possible to ask how the momentary solution will be different if the central bank, by finite open market transactions with the public which take zero time, alters the historically determined supplies of its monetary and non-monetary liabilities. The asset stock balance equations of the model—the LM locus in its simplest versions—shift to give the answer. But there is one slight difficulty with this scenario, rarely noticed in application of the model. The central bank is not free to engineer instantaneously, via open market operations, any finite change it desires in the state variables representing outstanding stocks of its liabilities. To issue a new dollar of base money, the central bank must buy already outstanding bonds at some market price. Presumably this price is the one that corresponds to the interest rate system the solution will throw up

---

Monetary Policy on Aggregate Demand," in J. L. Stein, ed., *Monetarism*, North-Holland, Amsterdam, 1976.

for the asset stocks outstanding *after* the operation. At this price the wealth state of the public will not be the same as if the operation did not occur. In the example, an increase in base money, it will generally be greater. If propensities to consume and save depend on wealth, the operation shifts the IS curve as well as the LM curve. (It is true that built into the IS curve may be the capital gains effects of variation of interest rate, but these are for given values of government liabilities, not for the changes accompanying open market operations.)

Some writers prefer to imagine variation of monetary stock by sudden helicopter drop of newly minted currency, rather than by central bank transactions in the market. This is a fairy tale way of packing a finite amount of deficit spending into an instant, as if your car suddenly jumped a kilometer ahead on the road. A drop of government bonds would, by analogy, achieve an instant increase in non-monetary debt. Here it is obvious that the public's wealth is suddenly increased, along with their specific holdings of the manna from heaven, and equally clear that completion of the story entails shifting IS as well as LM.

The momentary "point-in-time" interpretation of the Keynesian model and its IS/LM version, strictly adhered to, renders meaningless any dynamic analysis of its own solution. If the solution isn't a durable equilibrium, it can't be the steady state of another dynamic system. It *is* the dynamic system, or rather the momentary stage of a dynamic process. So on this interpretation it doesn't make sense to regard the multiplier embedded in the model as an infinite-series process in time, or to apply Samuelson's correspondence principle to the Keynesian model,[7] or to

---

[7] P. Samuelson, *Foundations of Economic Analysis*, Harvard University Press, Cambridge, 1947, p. 258.

draw à la Hicks phase diagrams in IS/LM space.[8] We must also eschew the use of stability considerations to limit the configurations to which we apply comparative static analysis. If the solution of the model itself gives the values of its variables at every moment of time, its structural equations should already include the adjustment lags considered in the stability analyses cited. Specifying the structural equations and drawing the curves with this in mind might, it is true, give them different shapes, slopes, and shifts from those to which equilibrium thinking has accustomed us.

Stability analysis of the IS/LM model, then, can be rationalized only by taking an equilibrium rather than a momentary view of the model's solution. But then, according to my previous argument, there is some inconsistency in taking Keynesian "equilibrium" as the asymptotic result of a long process of adjustment while ignoring the stock accumulations or decumulations that are bound to occur during the process.

I turn now to some objections to interpreting the IS/LM solution as the momentary state of a dynamic process in continuous time. The first relates to the Walrasian Auctioneer, that prodigious goddess about whom I expressed some incredulity in previous lectures. The model is, after all, a set of interdependent simultaneous equations. Although our macro models have, in comparison with full-blown general equilibrium models, a trivial number of equations, we understand them to be an approximate representation of a true system with many, many more markets, equations and variables. So the skepticism of the previous lecture must be repeated. Solving these equations every micro-second seems an unbelievably heavy task for the Auctioneer.

---

[8] As in his *A Contribution to the Theory of the Trade Cycle*, Chapters XI and XII.

A second objection concerns the disparity in the model between saving and the specific components of saving. The saving function—or consumption function—tells at what rate households wish to be adding to their wealth. In the solution, it tells how fast they actually are adding to their wealth. However, the model does not tell at what rate they desire to add to their wealth in any specific form, money or bonds or capital or foreign assets. Rather the model contains equations, or in simplest version the single LM equation, one side of which describes how households wish to allocate their existing stock of wealth. Household portfolio preferences are specified with respect to stocks but not with respect to flows. Now the flows, the rates at which stocks are increasing, are of course modeled. They are modeled on the supply side, and only there. The solution tells, or can be made to tell, the rates at which capital, government debt in its various forms, and net foreign assets are changing. In the next solution of the model, at the next instant of time in a continuous process, households have a different stock of wealth and must allocate the whole stock again. Their portfolio preferences must be reconciled, by interest rates and other variables, to the changed supplies of the several assets available to them.

I do not think this story, which omits savers' demand functions for rates of increase in specific assets, commits logical error. After all, portfolio preferences do come through at the end of the story, when the new vector of asset stocks must find willing holders. However, the scenario implies an implausible degree of fluidity in portfolios. Every instant the allocation of the whole wealth of households is reconsidered. Given the final vector of stocks, the model implies, it does not matter by what time paths they reached their current values. Empirically, over the short run, at least, it seems that flows matter more than their proportion of stocks would indicate. There is likely some inertia in portfolio adjustment that is not captured by the standard IS/LM model.

Have I painted us into a corner? I have reported or raised objections to both interpretations of the IS/LM solution, stationary equilibrium and momentary state of a process in continuous time. What is an alternative? Before I describe one, I want to repeat a statement I made at the beginning of the lecture. I do not think that the objections make the model, interpreted either way, useless or the lessons commonly derived from it wrong. On the contrary, I think that the model is a very instructive analytical and pedagogical tool. But, like most of the abstractions of our so-called science, it needs to be used with discretion and wisdom, and with understanding of its limitations. Moreover, I suggest, those who apply it and teach it should be clear about which interpretation fits best the context and the problem at hand.

An alternative is a discrete-time framework. Time is not continuous but broken into periods of finite duration. In any one period each of the simultaneously determined endogenous variables assumes one and only one value. Over a period of finite length flows add finite amounts to stocks. Saving during the period makes wealth larger at the end of the period; net investment adds to the capital stock; government budget deficits add to public debt; current account surpluses add to net foreign assets. In deciding their consumption, their investment, and their demands for specific assets, economic agents are determining their end-of-period stocks. Their behavior takes this into account. Thus there are explicit specific saving functions for each asset, adding up to total saving desired. The government budget identity is explicitly respected. Money and bonds issued to finance the deficit must be willingly absorbed into savers' portfolios, at the values of interest rates, income, and other variables determined for the period. The same is true of securities, bonds or equities, issued to finance private capital formation. Central bank operations in securities or foreign exchange markets can be easily modeled as additions to demands or supplies in the relevant markets. Their transactions too must take place at the interest rates, exchange rates, asset prices determined by the model's solution for the period.

Modeled in this way, a discrete-time Keynesian IS/LM model can account, at least qualitatively, for some phenomena which the equilibrium or continuous-time versions either omit or consign to dynamic analysis. The discrete-time IS and LM curves, or their equivalent, encompass effects which in the continuous-time version can be displayed only by shifting the curves as stocks change and tracking the moving solutions. Of course, the discrete-time solution too is only a temporary state; the new stocks will generally lead to a different solution next period. As before, the only real equilibrium is the stationary or steady balanced growth state.

The discrete time approach has its own implausibilities. If it strains credulity to imagine simultaneous market clearings repeated every instant, it certainly is arbitrary to require the Auctioneer to clear each and every market on the same periodic schedule. We know from casual observation that some prices move virtually continuously, others less frequently, irregularly, and on diverse schedules. Modeling that complex aspect of reality is a task I shall have to leave to younger generations. Meanwhile, we must recognize that either treatment of time is an imperfect and unrealistic representation of simultaneous and intertemporal interdependence. We had better avoid dogmatism in favor of either method. One practical advantage of discrete-time modeling is that it is inevitably the procedure used in empirical work, whether structural equations or complete macro models.

In the remaining part of the lecture I shall be more precise and specific about the structure of discrete-time macro models.

A Framework for Macroeconomic Models of Asset Accumulation

The accounting framework is simple. Consider a "flow of funds" matrix of which rows (indexed by capital letters) represent assets (like currency, government bonds, equities, deposits), while columns (indexed by lower-case letters) represent sectors of the economy (like households, businesses, governments, banks, rest of the world). An entry x_{Ss} then represents the net purchases of asset S by sector s during a particular time. A negative entry means net sales. If the matrix describes completely a closed system, each row must sum to zero. A row accounts for all sectors' sales and purchases of a particular item, and they must balance. A column accounts for a single sector's purchases and sales of all assets, and its total is the sectors' net saving or dissaving in the list of assets during the period. The format can accommodate any desired degree of disaggregation, varying the number of sectors and items.

The accounting framework comes to life as an economic model when the entries x_{Ss}, at least some of them, become variables to be explained by the behavior of the sector. The rows are then interpreted as asset markets, and the zero sums of these row equations become conditions determining the values of some variables rather than mere *ex post* accounting identities. In general a matrix for N assets will provide N equations and permit their simultaneous solution for N variables. These are the within-period endogenous variables of the model. Each one of these variables is assumed to take on one and only one value each period, a value determined during that period. Shortly I will be more concrete in identifying the within-period endogenous variables.

For the household sector, the column sum is household *Saving*. For the business sector, it is the negative of business Investment; that is, net sales of financial assets by businesses during a period finance their net acquisitions of real capital assets. For government, the sum is the Surplus, or minus the Deficit. Governments' net sales of assets finance the budget deficit; this is the famous government budget identity. For banks and other financial intermediaries, the column sums are zero. For the rest of the world, net purchases on capital account sum to the country's deficit on current account.

Thus the row—the $(N+1)$st row—obtained by summing the N asset rows equations is the familiar national accounting identity: household *Saving* equals the sum of net domestic *Investment*, the government *Deficit*, and the current account *Balance*. When the items in this row are, like those in the rows of which it is the sum, functions of the variables of the system, this row too is an equation, not just an identity. Indeed it is the IS locus. But it is not an additional independent equation. For every vector of the endogenous "unknowns" of the system, the IS equation is just the summation of the specific asset equations. Any one of the $N+1$ equations can be dropped for purposes of analysis. The symmetrical procedure appears to be to drop the IS locus, as radical a departure from convention as this may seem to be.

Earlier in the lecture I discussed the spirit motivating the approach. It is to provide a specific equation for each asset in form similar to the general saving/investment equation. That is, household saving in any asset S equals the amount of investment financed by business sales of asset S plus the amount of the government deficit so financed plus the amount of the asset sold by foreigners to finance the country's current account surplus.

Here then is a generalized row, for asset S:

$$(6) \qquad x_{Sh} = -x_{Sb} - x_{Sg} - x_{Sf} - x_{Sw}$$

where h, b, g, f, w refer respectively to households, business, government, financial intermediaries, and rest of world. Let I represent business net investment, D the government deficit, and B the current account balance. It is realistic and convenient to model business and government behavior as follows:

$$(7) \qquad -x_{Sb} = \beta_S I + b_S, \quad \sum_S b_S = 0, \quad \sum_S \beta_S = 1, \quad 0 \leqslant \beta_S \leqslant 1$$

$$(8) \qquad -x_{Sg} = \gamma_S D + g_S, \quad \sum_S g_S = 0, \quad \sum_S \gamma_S = 1, \quad 0 \leqslant \gamma_S \leqslant 1$$

The coefficients β_S are the proportions of investment financed by issuing various business securities. The coefficients γ_S are the proportions of the deficit the government finances by issues of its various liabilities, money and interest-bearing time obligations. The b_S represent refinancing of existing business liabilities and equity. Likewise, the g_S represent government exchanges of base money and debt instruments, and debt management operations replacing one kind or outstanding debt with another. Naturally these entries will be zero in many cells. Government does not enter the market for business equities, for example.

It is not so obviously appropriate to describe in this manner foreigners' sales of foreign assets to domestic wealth owners, or foreigners' sales of previously acquired obligations of the domestic sectors. It is not so natural to think of these transactions as geared to the rest-of-the-world's deficit B to the home country. But the model does need a balance-of-payments equation. Suppose that we group all the world assets available to domestic sectors in one row $(S = W)$, as would be appropriate if their foreign-currency prices and interest rates were all exogenous to the economy being modeled. Then the row for this asset is the balance of payments equation, as follows:

$$(9) \qquad x_{Wh} + x_{Wb} + x_{Wg} + x_{Wf} = B + \sum_{S \neq W} x_{Sw}$$

In words, domestic asset-holders earn foreign assets by running a current account surplus, or acquire them when foreigners buy domestic assets in exchange.

Households are aiming for end-of-period stocks of value h^S in terms of consumption goods at prices of the period. These are functions $h^S(\cdot)$ of current-period variables—interest rates and expected asset yields, incomes, taxes, etc.—and of state variables determined before the period. The latter include households' beginning-of-period asset stocks S^h_{-1}. Part of their end-of-period stock demand is, of course, met by those initial stocks, valued at the asset prices (in consumption goods) of the period, q_S. The remainder of the h^S (conceivably negative) must be acquired by purchases (or sales) during this period. Specific household saving in asset S is:

$$(10) \qquad x_{Sh} = h^S(\cdot) - q_S S^h_{-1}$$

Total household saving is accordingly:

$$(11) \qquad \sum_S x_{Sh} = \sum_S h^S(\cdot) - \sum_S q_S S^h_{-1}$$

Portfolio choice and saving are simultaneous and integrated decisions. The same list of arguments appear in $(\cdot)$ in the specific asset demand functions in (10) and in overall wealth demand in (11).

To put the same point another way, desired accumulation of a single asset, or of all assets together, refers to the differences between end-of-period real value and beginning-of-period real value. One component of this difference is capital gain or loss, the change in the value of the initial holding because of rise or fall in real asset price. The remainder is saving, the asset purchases households must make to meet their goals for accumulation. The assumption in (10) and (11) is that saving schedules for the period, in relation to asset prices, take full account of appreciations of existing holdings associated with each vector of asset prices. Such dollar-for-dollar fungibility between asset purchases and capital gains may be unrealistic. Household portfolios may adjust to capital gains and losses only partially within the period they occur, remaining adjustments occurring later. It would be possible to modify the specification in this direction.

For most assets the current real price q_s varies inversely with the corresponding real interest rate r_s, the yield expected from holding the asset until next period. For base money and for bank deposits payable on demand the nominal asset price is identically 1, the real price q_s is the reciprocal of the commodity price $1/P$, and the real interest rate is in effect the negative of the expected inflation rate. The assumption is that the nominal interest on these demand assets is legally or institutionally fixed at zero or some other ceiling rate. For foreign assets, whose yield and price are taken to be fixed exogenously in foreign currency, the real domestic asset price is proportional to e/P where e is the price of foreign currency, the exchange rate.

The portfolio adjustments of other sectors may be modeled analogously to those of households, except that those of government would be taken as exogenous in an analysis of fiscal, financial, and monetary policies. We would expect stable asset demand functions of foreigners $w^s(\cdot)$ to be expressed in their own currencies and consumption goods. Thus we would have to multiply them by ePW/P to convert them into home-country real values commensurable with other entries in the rows.

The existing capital stock K_{-1} is assumed to be held entirely by business. In the absence of business debt and business holdings of other financial assets, each physical unit of capital stock would be represented by an equity claim. Then Pq_EE_{-1} would be the share market valuation of a capital stock whose replacement cost at current commodity prices is PK_{-1}. The real valuation q_E will be inversely related to r_E, the one-period market yield from holding equity, and positively related to R_K, the real earnings yielded by productive operation of the capital stock. Investment adding K to the capital stock is—still assuming 100%-equity firms—financed by issue of new equity of real value $q_E\triangle K$, whether explicitly by sale of new securities or implicitly by equivalent retention and reinvestment of earnings.

Business capital accumulation K, as a proportion of the existing capital stock K_{-1}, is an increasing function of q_E. The symbol I refers to $q_E\triangle K$, and it too is an increasing function of q_E. High values of q_E, associated with relatively low market equity yield r_E and relatively high internal rate of return R_K, encourage businesses to undertake high rates of investment. Adjustment costs incident to capital accumulation rise with the rate of investment. Businesses must incur these costs in addition to the normal prices of the commodities they are installing as productive capital. That is why it takes abnormally high values of q_E—above 1—to encourage exceptionally high speeds of investment. Thus I is the proper measure of resources used for current investment, even though the resulting addition to the productive capital stock K may be a smaller amount. Likewise, when q is low—less than 1—there will be disinvestment in a stationary economy or investment that increases the capital stock less than the normal trend in a growing economy.[9]

Things are a bit more complicated when account is taken of business use of debt finance. According to the Modigliani–Miller theorem, the asset-market value of the capital stock q_K is independent of the debt/equity ratio, or more generally, of the structure of business finance.[10] Thus businesses can be modeled as if they are pure equity firms. The theorem goes much too far, in my opinion, but that is a subject beyond my current scope. In any case, q_K is a weighted average of q_E and the q's of other instruments used to finance business capital holdings. Investment can be related to q_K, even though this valuation depends in turn on existing financial structure and on the real yields on all the financial instruments in use.

Modeling financial intermediary sectors—banks and other institutions—involves several variations of the general structure so described. During a period, these institutions buy a vector x_{Sf} of business, government, household, and foreign liabilities; some of these entries are of course

---

[9] On the "q" theory of investment, see:

J. Tobin, "A General Equilibrium Approach to Monetary Theory," *Journal of Money, Credit, and Banking*, February 1969.

———, "Monetary Policy in 1974 and Beyond," *Brooking Papers on Economic Activity*, 1:1974.

——— and William C. Brainard, "Asset Markets and the Cost of Capital," R. Nelson and B. Balassa, eds., *Economic Progress: Private Values and Public Policy: Essays in Honor of W. Fellner*, North-Holland, Amsterdam, 1977.

J. Tobin, "Monetary Policies and the Economy: The Transmission Mechanism," *Southern Economic Journal*, January 1978.

[10] F. Modigliani and M. Miller, "The Cost of Capital, Corporation Finance, and the Theory of Investment," *American Economic Review*, June 1958.

negative and the total must be zero. (Strictly speaking, this condition cannot be met without explicit recognition of the equities of other sectors in the financial institutions.) For most assets, banks and other financial institutions can achieve the end-of-period stocks they desire at prevailing values of interest rates and other relevant variables. Among those stocks will be banks' liabilities on deposit accounts for which banks can bid by offering competitive yields. But this is not true of fixed-interest deposits. With effective nominal interest ceilings on deposits, banks passively accept as liabilities whatever the public chooses to deposit at the controlled rates. In such a row the bank column entry is simply the negative of the sum of the other entries, and banks' asset demands in other rows are constrained by this item. Indeed it is possible to eliminate fixed-interest deposits from the system, and to translate the fixed-interest deposit demands for other assets that arise from the banks' disposition of these deposits.

One of the asset rows is for base money, or high-powered money, as it is often called. In most monetary systems, base money is used as bank reserves and as circulating currency and coin. Banks' holdings of base money depend on their deposits. In many systems there are legal fractional reserve requirements. Reserves may exceed requirements, in amounts that depend on market interest rates and on the central bank's lending rate. For a system like that of the United States, it is convenient to regard bank borrowing from the central bank as a negative demand for base money, and to regard the supply of base money as excluding borrowed reserves. The flow of new base money during the period comes from partial or complete financing of the current government budget deficit by "printing" money, and from the central bank's open market purchases of domestic assets or of foreign-currency assets.

What are the N variables for which a system of this

structure may be solved, either by the model builder or by the Walrasian Auctioneer? There are numerous possibilities, among them the following:

1. *Flexible exchange rates, predetermined price levels and expected inflation rate.* (The assumption is only that the price level today and the price level expected for tomorrow are not endogenous within the current period. They do not have to be the same from period to period. They can be state variables, like asset stocks, moving "between periods" in accordance with what happened in the last and previous periods.)

The N within-period endogenous variables include at most $N-1$ interest rates r_s or equivalently $N-1$ variable asset prices q_s, which are inversely related to the interest rates. One of these asset prices, that for foreign assets, is simply the real exchange rate e/P. There may be other assets, like fixed-interest deposits, on which interest rates are fixed; in these cases, as explained above, there is an endogenous quantity instead of an endogenous price or interest rate. But there remains one asset equation, that for base money, for which there is no corresponding endogenous interest rate or quantity. Thus there is room for an Nth endogenous variable, and the natural choice is real net national product Y.

The exogenous or predetermined variables include: the parameters of governmental fiscal policy which help to determine the deficit D, namely real government purchases G and the tax-transfer function $T(Y)$, perhaps $T_0 + tY$; the parameters γ_s determining how the deficit is financed; the open market monetary and debt management transactions of the central bank and government m_s, including interventions in the foreign asset markets m_w; foreign-currency interest rates, asset prices, and commodity prices; initial asset holdings of each sector.

2. *Fixed exchange rate, predetermined price level and expected inflation rate.* Fixing e eliminates an endogenous variable. The natural replacement is m_W, central bank purchases of foreign assets. The remaining m_S are then constrained to add to $-m_W$. The customary convention—no "sterilization"—is that base money is issued to buy foreign assets, but this is not the only possibility. With this change, the structure of the model is like case (1).

3. *Supply-determined output.* The positions of Y and P can be interchanged in either exchange rate regime. Then we have a "classical" rather than a "Keynesian" system, with output in full Walrasian equilibrium and prices sufficiently flexible within the period to keep it there.

4. *Within-period Phillips curve.* The previous regimes can be modified to allow both output and price to be endogenous within a period, provided an extra equation describing their temporary tradeoff is appended.

What are the analytical conclusions? This is not the time or place for exercises in comparative statics. In a series of papers available elsewhere, I and my collaborators have carried out a number of such exercises.[11] At the beginning

---

[11] J. Tobin and W. Buiter, "Long Run Effects of Fiscal and Monetary Policy on Aggregate Demand," in J. L. Stein, ed., *Monetarism*, North-Holland, Amsterdam, 1976.

J. Tobin, "Deficit Spending and Crowding Out in Shorter and Longer Runs," in H. L. Greenfield, *et al.*, *Theory for Economic Efficiency: Essays in Honor of Abba P. Lerner*, M.I.T. Press, Cambridge, 1979.

J. Tobin and W. Buiter, "Fiscal and Monetary Policies, Capital Formation, and Economic Activity," forthcoming in: George M. von Furstenberg, ed., *The Government and Capital Formation*, American Council of Life Insurance, 1979.

of this lecture, I anticipated one major general conclusion, namely the robustness of the standard results of Hicksian IS/LM analysis. They survive in these models in which time, flows, and stocks are more precisely and satisfactorily modeled, in which time is allowed for flows to affect the stocks of government liabilities and of other assets too, in which the menu of distinct assets is as large as desired.

By standard results, I have in mind propositions like the following:

a   expansionary fiscal policies—increases in G or tax reductions—raise output Y and/or price P, whatever the vector of (non-negative) γs determining the financing of budget deficits, whether the exchange rate is floating or fixed; they generally also raise real interest rates relevant to investment decisions and displace some investment;

b   expansionary monetary and financial policies—open market purchases of other assets with base money, or shifts of γs towards monetary financing of deficits —generally raise output Y and/or price P while lowering interest rates relevant to investment decisions and "crowding in" some investment; these qualitative results also apply in both exchange rate regimes.

Sufficient assumptions for these standard results are not very restrictive, but they are not necessarily met. The most important are these:

a   In the end-of-period portfolio demands of each sector, the assets are gross substitutes. That is, an increase in an asset's one-period yield increases the demand for that

---

J. Tobin and J. B. de Macedo, "The Short-Run Macroeconomics of Floating Exchange Rates: An Exposition," forthcoming in J. Chipman and C. Kindleberger, eds., *Flexible Exchange Rates and the Balance of Payments: Essays in Memory of Egon Sohmen.*

asset, and possibly for total wealth, but not for any other asset.

b   There is at least one asset to which demand for base money by some sector is negatively related.

c   At any vector of interest rates, an increase in Y or P raises household saving S more than it raises I+D+B. Also, an increase in Y or P raises specific saving in base money, and by more than it diminishes specific saving in any one other asset.

d   There is some inelasticity in exchange rate expectations, so that the domestic currency return on foreign assets is believed to be greater the lower the current exchange rate e.

e   The current account balance B in home currency varies directly with e/P—the Marshall–Lerner condition.

f   Since interest rate variations cause capital gains or losses on initial asset holdings which reinforce gross substitute properties when initial holdings are positive but oppose them when initial holdings are negative, the assumption is that any perverse effects are weaker than the substitution effects of interest rate variation. As observed in the first lecture, this assumption might be violated when price deflation increases debt burdens. An international example of the same phenomenon is that exchange rate depreciation will have perverse wealth effects on debtor countries.

Although models of this type in some sense "vindicate" IS/LM analysis, this is not their sole or principal purpose. Their richer structural detail permits the analysis of policies and exogenous shocks for which more primitive and more highly aggregated models are ill-suited. The vector of endogenous variables is also larger, and in particular effects on financial prices and quantities can be traced. A project with which I am associated at the Cowles Foundation for Research in Economics at Yale University is trying to build an empirical model of United States asset markets along the lines of the theoretical model I have described here.

The comparative statics of one-period solutions is, of course, far from the full story. The dynamic process is easy to describe in principle but hard to analyze and implement in practice. The solution of the current period determines the state variables for the next period, notably the stocks of assets and their distribution among sectors. These, together with the exogenous variables, both policy settings and other shocks, determine the next period solution.

In a steady state, if one exists, interest rates and asset prices are constant, government policy settings are stable, real stocks and flows are growing at a common natural rate, and nominal quantities are growing at the same rate plus a constant actual and expected rate of inflation. This inflation rate is also the negative of the real rate of interest on base money; an important difference between short-run and long-run macroeconomics is that in the long run equilibrium the real rate of return on base money is, like other real rates of interest, endogenous. Other important differences, of course, are that the capital stock is endogenous in the long run and that both labor and capital services are fully employed. In the third lecture, the steady state solution of a model of this type was discussed, with particular reference to the relation of fiscal and financial policies to inflation rates and capital intensity.

Index